JUDGMENT DAY

JUDGMENT DAY

BOB LANCASTER & B.C. HALL

SEAVIEW/PUTNAM
NEW YORK

Library of Congress Cataloging in Publication Data

Lancaster, Bob.
  Judgment day.

1.   Murder—Missouri—Skidmore—Biography.
2.   McElroy, Ken Rex. 3. Crime and criminals—
Missouri—Skidmore—Biography.   4. Sex crimes—
Missouri—Skidmore.   5. Victims of crime—Missouri—
Skidmore.   I. Hall, B. Clarence, date. II. Title.
HV6534.S55L36 1983 364.1'523'0924 [B] 82-80381
ISBN 0-399-31015-0

Printed in the United States of America

Acknowledgments

The authors wish to thank the following people for all their help and support: Nick Ellison, Mike Hamilburg, Tucker Steinmetz, Joe Stocks, Nita Webb, Bobby and Antoinette Zimmerman—and Daphna and Martha.

To the memory of Black Hawk,
the last Nodaway Emperor

Contents

"Most people believe the killing was justified. And you know why? They probably
had never seen this man McElroy in their
lives, but they want to believe such a story.
There is no way you can justify the taking
of a life, but people want to believe there is
some hope against beasts . . ."
—Father Alphonse of the
Conception Monastery in
Nodaway County, Missouri

JUDGMENT DAY

The Road to Skidmore

SKIDMORE, July 10, 1981—Ken Rex McElroy, 47, of Skidmore, Missouri, was dead-on-arrival today at St. Francis Hospital in Maryville after a shooting incident in downtown Skidmore.

First reports of the incident said a crowd of about sixty Skidmore residents was on the scene at the time of the killing. Medical examiners in Maryville reported that McElroy was shot in the back of the head with a high powered rifle.

An investigation is now underway. No arrests have been made, Nodaway County officials said. Skidmore is a small farming community of about four hundred people in the northwest corner of Missouri.

JUDGMENT DAY

McElroy was born June 16, 1934, in Quitman, six miles north of Skidmore. The son of Tony Wyatt and Mabel Lister McElroy, he owned a farm south of Skidmore and was a coon-dog breeder.

He is survived by his wife, Trena, and his mother. Other survivors include five sons, six daughters, six brothers, six sisters, and one grandson.

A private service will be held Tuesday at Price Funeral Home, Maryville, and burial will be in Memorial Park, St. Joseph.

—Obituary of Ken Rex McElroy

The road to Skidmore starts wherever you are. Just point yourself toward the very heart of America and that's the road.

It's a long old road which leads near the end into Kansas City, the hub of the farm belt and the great American jumping-off place. It would be a good idea to linger there in Kansas City, as Lewis and Clark did, as the pioneers did, before plunging off on the last leg of the journey into the unknown.

"If you want to see some sin," Edward R. Murrow once wrote, "forget about Paris and go to Kansas City. With the possible exception of Singapore or Port Said, Kansas City has the greatest sin industry in the world."

It was a wicked, crooked, lively city in the days of the

speakeasy and the striptease, of Count Basie and "Pretty Boy" Floyd. But no more. The old corruption is still there, but it operates now behind a mask of dull respectability.

The city seems as contemporary and banal as the Hallmark greeting cards it turns out by the millions, as bland as the open midwestern face of its favorite third baseman, George Brett of the Royals.

Ernest Hemingway once compared Kansas City to Constantinople. He didn't explain, but he must have had in mind that both cities are famous gateways—the "gateway to the West," the "gateway to the Orient." Crossroads cities where all the twains meet, where all the influences converge and rub off a little as they pass through. Cities that easterners think of as western and westerners think of as eastern, and northerners think of as southern and southerners think of as northern. And they're all right, and all wrong.

The influence of Harry Truman can still be felt in Kansas City, and it is in Kansas City that the influence of Kenneth Rex McElroy, the central figure in this story of blood and terror, first makes itself felt.

Ken Rex, he was called—the name means "handsome king." He came to Kansas City often, especially in those last turbulent years. His lawyer was in Kansas City and Ken Rex needed a lawyer the way chronically sick people need a doctor. Everyone agreed that he had a good lawyer in that wicked old city that has become the "Happy Birthday" and "Get Well Soon" capital of the world.

Skidmore sometimes wondered why a lawyer that capable—with all the big-time connections he was supposed to have—would spend so much time and effort getting a boondocks bully like Ken Rex McElroy out of trouble. In the aftermath of Judgment Day, Skidmore would entertain itself with many rumors about the Ken Rex–Kansas City connection. One of those rumors was this:

Ken Rex had been overheard to brag that he was a hit man for the North Kansas City mob. Skidmore had always assumed that such bragging was just barstool guff, Ken Rex trying to impress somebody or deflect nosy questions about where he got all his money. But after Judgment Day, Skidmore wondered: Had anyone ever really heard him say he was a hit man? Could it have been true?

Like all the other unanswered questions, these rumors became a part of the Ken Rex legend, grist for the unfolding heartland myth.

From Kansas City the road to Skidmore is only 110 miles long. It heads north, crossing the wide Missouri and threading through grim North Kansas City. Next is a stretch of unremarkable Interstate for fifty miles to St. Joseph, but you sense having made the passage through the Kansas City gateway. The humpy terrain flattens as the land gets richer and more sure of itself. The soil blackens.

St. Joseph was also a famous jumping-off place once—a favorite departure point for the Forty-Niners and home base for the pony express and the Overland stage. There's no jumping off there now. The last pony express rider is bronze and so is his horse. The new migrants, the new nomads, use different routes, and St. Joseph is a settled, somnolent town of about 100,000, snuggled comfortably in the bosom of rich farmland that nurtures it. It looks clean, placid, wholesome, and, with its bewildering intersections, just a little absentminded—as if it might be the hometown of Walter Cronkite, which it is.

18

THE ROAD TO SKIDMORE

It's hard to believe that sweet old roly-poly St. Joe was once the home roost for the James gang, but it was. It was also one of the haunts of Ken Rex McElroy, who would become a criminal legend himself.

Ken Rex was said to have shot up a St. Joe tavern once in an effort to spook some would-be witnesses against him in one of his first felony cases. Although he was never convicted, Ken Rex was for years what the St. Joe police call a "known character"—that is, a character with no conviction record but one you damn sure better watch out for. When he was finally gunned down, his widow had him brought to St. Joe for burial, saying she couldn't stand the thought of putting him in the unwelcome ground near Skidmore, where so many people had hated his guts.

The road to Skidmore veers off the Interstate at St. Joe, heading north by northwest toward the very heart of the continental United States, entering the central plain where the Missouri cowlick brushes Iowa, Nebraska, and Kansas. It has come now into the most productive farmland on the face of the earth, which stretches from Lake Superior to the southwestern deserts, rolling west from here until it steppes up to the Rockies. This is America's breadbasket, with soil like granulated licorice. That soil made Nikita Khrushchev so envious when he visited the area a couple of decades ago that he threatened to bury us in it.

Ken Rex knew that soil well. He spent his whole life on it and called himself one of its farmers. But one has to wonder what it meant to him—if he felt the reverence for this land that the real farmers, including his farmer brothers, feel. No, the land had a hold on him, but he fought it, refused to conform or to behave, refused to submit to the unspoken conventions that the land imposes. He struggled against the hold of this land as though he knew that the land had a deadly curse on it—a curse he tempted, dared, defied, and taunted until Skidmore came to believe *he* was the curse.

No, this soil which rose up finally to take him back, to soak up his blood and recycle the scattered bits of his exploded brain, meant something different to him than to his brothers.

Living off the land meant something very different to him.

At Savannah, a small town eighteen miles out of St. Joe, the road to Skidmore narrows to two lanes. This is Highway 71, an ever-diminishing tributary of the Interstate. There's not much traffic and the road is a straight shot—maybe too straight. The bumper sticker of a passing car gives one pause:

I DRIVE HIGHWAY 71

PRAY FOR ME

Soon there comes along a stretch of tobacco farms, unique in this part of the world. Tobacco seems out of place here. As out of place as blacks, poodles, Moonies, pine trees, and one-story houses without sitting porches. As Ken Rex McElroy must have seemed out of place. It's hard to say why. Maybe it is that this land simply has its conventions, which are as precise and peculiar as New England's or Mississippi's, so that exceptions to the norm attract a lot of notice.

It's suddenly apparent that it's farther back from Savannah to Kansas City than the hour and a half it takes to drive. The buffalo used to run through here, and Kansas City, the gateway, seems as distant now as the buffalo.

The land has assumed a beautiful, soft undulation, a corrugation rippled up in advance of the Ice Age glaciers and smoothed down by millenniums of rain and wind and blowing dust. Its rolls lull you like surf.

Each time the road to Skidmore tops one of those rolls, you feel yourself perched on the rim of a huge saucer of land that might be several miles across. And then the road plunges into the swale of that saucer and there seems to be no other world behind or ahead on either side. The horizon is a circle; the landscape all around rises gently in the distance to meet the blue dome of sky.

It is a landscape of colorful intersecting planes, like the vistas of the Flemish masters—dark green fields of tall corn and bright green fields of low-lying soybeans, a swath of black earth, a gray slash of distant hardwoods, a tilted-back square of meadow, yellow and brown, dappled with slick black cattle and pink hogs.

That landscape means the road has entered Nodaway County, Skidmore's county. Ken Rex McElroy's county. The county where their dark struggle occurred and engendered an American myth.

The road tops one of those glacial rolls and slides down into the little city of Maryville, the county seat and the last fair-sized anchorage before the last tributary that leads to Skidmore itself.

Maryville, the scene of the aftermath where all the fact finders gathered, lodged, deliberated, and gave up, is a perky little town of about nine thousand people. Dale Carnegie, the author of *How to Win Friends and Influence People,* was a native of Maryville. His hometown is its own Dale Carnegie course: friendly, courteous, unpretentious, uninteresting, and shallow. It might just as easily be located in Maryland or Kentucky or Illinois, and it makes Kansas City seem not so far away.

Maryville has some industry—Union Carbide, Uniroyal

Tire, Regal Textiles ("the baby-diaper factory")—and a nice shopping center, along with a couple of small subdivisions with cookie-cutter houses. It has its tugs of war between Ronald McDonald and Colonel Sanders, between the Pizza Hut and the Dairy Queen. It has a kind of Holiday Inn, only it's in the guise of the Wilson Motel and the Hitching Post Restaurant. It has a small hospital, where Ken Rex was pronounced dead; it has two funeral homes, one of which disposed of Ken Rex's blasted remains; it has a small five-days-a-week newspaper, which held the presses for the Judgment Day murder scoop.

It also has Northwest Missouri State College, but the college, like the members-only Maryville Country Club, seems to have finer things to think about than all the melodrama out at Skidmore. The tragedy was too low-life; the larval myth reeked of honky-tonk and kicker coarseness. *Skidmore?* Ah, yes, the NWMS professor recalled, he used to leave his car in Skidmore when he went off trysting with his student sweetie.

The main thing Maryville has, as far as Skidmore is concerned, is the Nodaway County Courthouse, a looming turn-of-the-century Victorian edifice that you can see from miles away.

That courthouse provides a visitor with an excuse to tarry for a while in Maryville, just as those prairie-schooner immigrants tarried in Kansas City and St. Joe, readying their wagons and their wills. The courthouse is important because it was the third major character in the Skidmore drama. The journalists even came to regard it as the *main* character—the one that could have interposed itself between Ken Rex and Skidmore and thereby saved the day for truth, justice, and the American way. But when the crisis arose, the courthouse wasn't up to its role; it came to represent failure and fatuity—Pontius Pilate washing his bureaucratic hands of the whole messy affair.

Most courthouses burn down sooner or later, but the Nodaway County Courthouse never has. For generations it has squatted there as solid as one of the old forts in the badlands, in the wilds beyond the western frontier. But a courthouse is more than just a building, more than just a centerpiece for a town square. It's more than just its echoing old halls, its chambers of brass and polished wood, its airless little offices where taciturn deputies and clerks with beehive hairdos pass the days and years among musty ledgers and high cabinets crammed with forgotten documents. If it's anything, it's the embodiment of an idea, or really a whole web of vital ideas.

Without the courthouse and what it stands for, people would be marooned in their individual lives, with only the most tenuous connections to their ancestors and their heirs. Their claims to property, to basic rights, even to their names, would be arbitrary. The courthouse shelters deeds, court records, voting records, vital statistics—the papers of citizenship. The courthouse alone verifies that a person was born, lived, married, paid his taxes, and died.

But maybe the most crucial idea the courthouse embodies is the same one those wilderness forts embodied: that there is protection for civilization against lawlessness, disorder, injustice, and terrorism. And if people lose faith in the idea of the courthouse as such a bulwark, then civilization itself may recede—as Kansas City and St. Joe receded for those pioneers—and the consequent plunge into darkness can be a savage one.

So it was the failure of an idea that occurred in Nodaway County, Missouri, in 1981, with consequences that are scary as hell to contemplate. And they're even scarier upon discovering, during the stop at Maryville, that the failure wasn't unprecedented. There was another crisis and another failure exactly fifty years before. An anniversary item buried in the Maryville *Daily Forum* only hints at it ominously, roiling the Nodaway memory:

> TODAY IN HISTORY
> 1931
> Sheriff Harve England does not expect any mob violence on Monday when Raymond Gunn, 27-year-old confessed slayer of Velma Colter, will be arraigned in Circuit Court here, but he will be prepared to call out the National Guard if needed.

The newspaper and the chamber of commerce here, like their counterparts all over the country, are strong on boosterism, and they call the trade area they serve the "Nodaway Empire."

There's something awkward, faintly ironical in the sound of that. "Nodaway" suggests dozing off, and a nodding-away empire evokes an image not of bustling midwestern free enterprisers but of latter-day Rome under the inbred, wined-up Caesars. A nodding-away emperor would have been one of those superannuated imperial popes or any of a number of the sluggardly kings of France.

Actually, Nodaway doesn't mean sleepy. And it's not a redskin word meaning "placid," as the Genealogical Society here ventured in its report of a hundred years ago.

THE ROAD TO SKIDMORE

It's a Sac-Fox Indian word that meant "snake" or "enemy."

Probably Snake Empire or Enemy Empire isn't what the chamber of commerce wants to convey either, but anyhow it's been 150 years since there was anything around these parts that justly could have been called an empire. That old empire, which went the way of the bison and the carrier pigeon, took in this little wedge of northwest Missouri, much of Iowa, and a corner of present-day Minnesota. Its emperor was a man with the leadership ability to merit the title, the only man in American history to have a war named after him.

His name was Black Hawk, and the Nodaway Empire under his feathered lance wasn't a heavy entity bounded by forts and anchored by courthouses. It was an empire as light on the land as the wind and the dew; it imposed itself on the land not with the iron weight of the locomotive and the plow, but with a feathery tread, an empire as benign and troubling as the wolf's or the hawk's. Its people hunted the buffalo here. They planted corn here.

But their claims weren't recognized by the courthouse of the white people who soon encroached, so those claims were quickly extinguished.

Along with the claimants.

It makes one think again about the courthouse and what great powers and responsibilities it embodies and how important is the success or failure of the system of justice it represents.

Ken Rex McElroy used to sit in a little tavern called the Shady Lady, which fronts on the town square in Maryville. He sat there often, drinking beer and looking out across the street at the Nodaway County Courthouse.

25

JUDGMENT DAY

He still does.

Considering the fact that he still does, Enemy Empire doesn't seem all that inappropriate after all.

*

The county roads in Missouri are designated by letters rather than numbers, and the road out to Skidmore from Maryville is named V. It starts beside the golden arches of McDonald's on Maryville's main drag, zigzags past one of those homologous subdivisions, and proceeds through a series of right angles out into the countryside, always following the old grid section lines that marked the early homesteads.

After about five miles, somewhere near the little bridge over White Cloud Creek, the road lips another of those saucers and again negates the world beyond. Though the road hasn't yet reached halfway to Skidmore, the city of Maryville is already as distant as the buffalo.

The circular horizon is again a blue-green seam where tall corn meets cloudless sky. Atop the glacial roll, the landscape has the look of enameled porcelain. Then, when the road drops down again, the elephant-eye corn grows up so close that it's like moving along some curiously sunken passage, like the long hollow between the looming billows of the sea.

You can smell the corn ripening in the fields. You can smell the earth itself, richly bloated in a placenta-like ripeness. Everything alive seems to close in tighter, so that it's no metaphor to say that the people of this region are close to the land.

Along the roadway, woolly worms by the dozen make a desperate, inexplicable bid to squirm from one side of the road to the other. Most of them make it because the traffic is light. They keep coming. A solitary shrike studies them from a fencerow persimmon tree up ahead. The shrike sees a feast. He is called the butcher bird.

The V that is this road's name doesn't stand for anything. Maybe it will someday, because the myth is in the making, and myths like to play little tricks with the accouterments, imbuing them with capricious meanings: V for Violence. V for Vengeance. V for Vindication. For Victory.

Here's the one the Nodaway Empire hates: V for Vigilantes.

The road to Skidmore dips and rolls. The sweet aroma of corn yields for a moment to the unmistakable sour smell of hogs. Nodaway County is famous for its hogs. A sweeping meadow ahead is speckled with Black Angus cattle. The arresting perspective is Breughel's. The farmhouses are never closer to one another than a mighty shout, and they are good, clean, solid houses with venerable shade trees, good, sturdy barns, and a pleasing assortment of outbuildings pleasingly arranged—altogether a spacious, orderly tableau, wholesome and nostalgic, affirming the strapping country rhythms of Vachel Lindsay's "Bryan, Bryan, Bryan, Bryan."

Just before Skidmore there is a gravel side road that snakes away to the south. Down that road, after a few bends along the grid, was where Ken Rex lived. It is a Willa Cather Neighbor-Rosicky kind of road: The farms are well-kept, abundant and unpretentious, but down the road a few miles the places fall into ungainly blisters, and the land thickens with weeds instead of rich cropland. The McElroy place is deserted now, though there is still the sign in the yard: GUARD DOGS ON DUTY. A carving of a golden eagle, stopped in flight, stays on the house's portal, perhaps only as a sullen, undetected omen that now grows more obscure with each passing day.

But that side road is not on the way to Skidmore—it is meant only for those who have to take it, and even the fact-finders pass it by.

Skidmore comes suddenly into view. At first sight it appears to be a city on a hill. The town drapes one of those glacial rolls and the whole extent of it is visible at a glance, not a mile across in any direction. It looks as if it would fit snugly into one of those Maryville subdivisions, which are themselves small.

What is striking in the first glimpse of Skidmore is not what is there but what is not.

There are no industries shouldering up to the town, smoking its air or scarifying its earth or just sprawling there. No big businesses and no small ones. Not even a chicken house or feedlot or abattoir.

There is no skyline. Not a building taller than the trees. Not a clock tower or steeple or water tank or grain silo or radio transmitter to disrupt the circular horizon.

There is no commercial development stripping any of the three roads leading into town. Not a single outlying place of business: not a diner, not a produce stand, not a gasoline station. Not even a billboard. Local color is courtesy of God.

Most out-of-the-way settlements have a transition zone where countryside gradually becomes transformed into streetside—a sequence of speed-limit signs, if nothing else, coercing the traveler into an annoyed acknowledgment of the existence of the place. Not Skidmore. There

28

is no edge-of-town buffer around Skidmore. You go directly from cornfields to Main Street, with only two discreet road signs to mark the passage.

One of these signs announces that the Missouri Betterment Association, working through the Skidmore Betterment Association, has applied itself here. It is reassuring to know that a place which looks so idle and hauntingly still is involved in a community betterment campaign. But that word "betterment" has taken on new and controversial shades of meaning since the sign went up. Did Skidmore better itself on July 10, 1981? Most of the townspeople would say that it did, and they could point to congratulatory letters from all over the country agreeing with them. But they would admit that the Judgment Day betterment was a species that the boosters of the Nodaway Empire wouldn't want to feature in their brochures.

The other sign says that Skidmore is the home of the annual Punkin Festival. (That's punkin, not pumpkin— with the down-home *n* sound in the middle that no doubt agitates some of the profs at Maryville.) Skidmore would say everyone should already know about its Punkin Festival without the sign. A late-summer harvest celebration with most of the ingredients of a county fair, the festival is Skidmore's big deal, its claim to fame. At least it *was.* In the summer of 1981 Skidmore was overrun with would-be fact finders—reporters, investigators, film crews, the morbidly curious—who didn't give a damn about any Punkin Festival.

Some of them were still around in late August for the festival, and you might suppose they threw a pall over the celebration. After all, it had been only six weeks since Judgment Day, and Skidmore was still in the news as Vigilante City, USA. The courthouse at Maryville was still noisily posturing as the redoubt of inevitable and retributive justice. The legendary Ken Rex was still on the street, in the glass and gore, festering in the noonday sun.

But no, there was no gloom at the 1981 Punkin Festival. Skidmore enjoyed it more than it had enjoyed a festival in a long time. In spite of the judgmental looks from the strangers. In spite of the noise about an imminent grand jury investigation. In spite of the melancholy shade of a murdered legend.

There was a good feeling in the air as people wandered among the flea-market stalls, watched the old-timers thwart the young bucks in the horseshoe-pitching duels, rooted for this or that contestant in the baby show or the Punkin Queen Contest, clapped for the square dancers as they do-si-doed to the yeehah music of the local band, Greg Clement and the Rednecks.

The good feeling was the same as that at a hundred harvest festivals in the small towns of the Midwest, only more so. But it was extraordinary at Skidmore and the reason why would have been obvious to anyone who had been at the Punkin Festival just a year before.

That was a time of unspoken terror in Skidmore—a terror that was becoming pervasive. And one night during the festival, in the shadows just beyond the hoopla, the popular young town marshal of Skidmore, Dave Dunbar, found himself with a 12-gauge shotgun poked in his gut and looking into the cold eyes of the source of that terror. For twenty minutes Dave Dunbar stood there, honestly not knowing from one breath to the next whether Ken Rex McElroy would pull the trigger.

The suspense of that twenty minutes in the shadows was a concentrate of the scary and steadily intensifying suspense that practically the whole community was coming to feel. By the time of the 1981 festival, Skidmore had delivered itself of that scourge, and its people had no apologies for and no regrets about the good feeling that was in the air.

So the road to Skidmore, with the scantest of transitions, becomes the main street of Skidmore. It has the look and feel of a small-town main street of seventy-five years ago, straight out of *Our Town*. It is canopied by big old maples and sycamores that put on a gorgeous show in the fall and it is lined with plain, clean, old-fashioned wood-frame Harry Truman houses, most of them two-storied, with roomy sitting porches.

The houses are built close to the street, as houses were when streets were safe and civilized, so there are no lawns to speak of. That was the way, too, in the presuburban days when lawns were called yards and were useful rather than decorative, when children romped in them, often among chickens, dogs, cats, sometimes a goat.

The main street of Skidmore has no sidewalks—the street is broad enough to accommodate both autos and pedestrians, though both are few and far between. The traffic is mainly an occasional pickup truck, and its driver is likely to raise an index finger from the steering wheel in greeting as he passes—a restrained but neighborly kind of wave, courteous but noncommittal.

This main street yields some clues about the nature of the people who inhabit the town. The street has no mansions and no hovels, no ostentation and no squalor, no cramping and no isolation, no racket and no litter. All of which suggests that Skidmore's population, which numbers right around four hundred, is pretty much one class of people: small-town, old-fashioned, outgoing midwesterners who wouldn't be offended if you called them middle-class.

There's also a hint of loneliness about the street—not much, but enough to suggest a community that is close-knit but whose people, nonetheless, with that personal solitude that is a poignant characteristic of the midwestern temper, keep their social relations relatively superficial, harboring their gravest concerns and dealing with them as best they can alone. That might have been an element in the evolution of the Skidmore tragedy. It might have been the reason that the people here took so long to get their act together against Ken Rex, to pool their collective outrage and become a single character with one mind, a character as formidable as the legendary antagonist, and willing to take him on at last. That character was the Skidmore that the world heard about.

After the equivalent of maybe seven city blocks, the street again changes character as it enters the tiny Skidmore business district. The end of the road to Skidmore is now in sight.

First, to the right, is the Skidmore Methodist church, a ponderous old thing of dark brick which hulks but fails to impress. Its pastor in 1981 was a young circuit rider named Mike Smith who lived and spent most of his time in Maitland, the next town south, six miles away but as distant as Maryville or St. Joe. As distant almost as Cape Girardeau, way down in the southeast corner of the state, where Mike Smith comes from and where they speak with southern accents. It was Mike who conducted the funeral service for Ken Rex, and who nearly got himself shot for going to the trouble.

Just past the church, across the street on the left, is Skidmore's dinky red-brick city hall and fire station, which functions primarily to shelter the municipal office and the fire truck, whose volunteer crew doesn't get many calls. Then, still on the left, there's the restored Skidmore depot, painted red—a memento from the days when Skidmore had a railroad—with a refurbished boxcar, painted blue, immobilized beside it, looking for all the world as if it would like to get the hell out of there and go back to work.

It's just a block farther now to the T-shaped intersection where the long road to Skidmore finally ends. Up the stem of that T, on the right, there is a single dilapidated storefront, browned by generations of prairie dust. It has an abandoned look. Grass grows through the crumbling concrete of its front step. A local farmer uses the biggest part of it to hangar some of his farm machinery, leaving a nook at one end for the post office and one at the other for a fledgling community library operated sporadically and informally by (and mostly for) some of the Skidmore womenfolk.

The weary old storefront faces three unconnected buildings across the street. The first, just past the blue boxcar, is Mom's Cafe, a dawn-to-dusk diner and popular meeting place for coffeeing and socializing. If poetry lived in the midwestern heart, the beer tavern next door to Mom's would be named Pop's. But it's called D&G's. There are always two or three pickups parked in front of D&G's. Ken Rex's big old cruiser with the mud flaps and gun rack had been there a thousand times. The last building on that side—up on the corner in the armpit of the T—is the doughty and prosperous little First American Bank of Skidmore, Ken Hurner president. Hurner is a hardworking, looked-up-to businessman, one of the influential civic leaders in Skidmore.

JUDGMENT DAY

It is the tavern, D&G's, that commands attention here at the end of the road. Because that tavern is the maelstrom's eye around which the growing myth swirls. It's there, all right, but it has another existence too—as a set piece in the mind, the eternal backdrop for a dead man slumped grotesquely in a bullet-riddled pickup, surrounded by a streetful of mute onlookers.

D&G's is an unlikely candidate for mythical status. It certainly isn't an imposing structure, at least from the exterior view. From the street it looks as though two crazy ne'er-do-wells who had salvaged some scrap sheet metal from a deserted construction site might have thrown it together in a single afternoon. Skidmore folks, both men and women, have a fondness for the place; they don't call it a bar or tavern but refer to it as "the poolhall."

But inside, it has a measure of authentic, though Spartan charm, reminiscent of the shotgun saloons of the boomtowns of the West, with a talkative bartender named Red Smith, who might not have been able to keep the jukebox out but who has the admirable sense to keep it unplugged.

At first it might seem odd that there's even a tavern in Skidmore. A teeny churchgoing town in the conservative, rural Midwest, without even a laundromat or a pharmacy, yet supporting a tavern? A tavern seems out of place here, like those tobacco fields. But Missourians, who gave the world Budweiser, have always liked their suds, and not even their small-towners ever had much use for the saloon smashers and temperance fanatics who dried up neighboring Kansas and Iowa in the prod for national Prohibition. One of the first white settlers in Nodaway County was a crusty Alabamian named Hiram Hall who among other pursuits peddled an elixir called Hall's Tonic. And ever

34

since, farmers of the Nodaway Empire have cherished the tradition of washing the cornfield dust out of their craws at the end of the day.

Thus the road to Skidmore ends, and any stranger who had been there at its terminus, at that T-shaped intersection on the morning of July 10, 1981—loitering there on the corner as Skidmore's youngsters do—would have been close enough for the concussion to ring in his ears, and might have come away with a powder burn. He might have been able to tell the authorities something that nobody else was able to tell them, or was willing to tell them. He might thereby have preserved little Skidmore's anonymity, spiking a good mystery and turning an American tragedy into routine journalism.

Who did it? Why?

The simple answers to those simple questions were here on this desolate street corner that morning. But they got away. Time passed. And even if those answers were retrievable now, they wouldn't matter anymore.

Because a bigger, meaner question—too big and too mean for anything but a genuine myth—moved into the void that all the factfinders couldn't fill:

What did it mean?

There's more to Skidmore, but not much more.

After a block on either arm of that T, the Skidmore business district poops out.

The right arm wears the "town square" atop its shoulder—an empty lot really, with a few trees and shrubs. But then it elbows quickly, bringing into view a rundown Highway Department maintenance shed, with the old Skidmore schoolhouse, long since consolidated into a county district, languishing in the background. Then it drops down the glacial roll past the Christian church (Reverend Tim Warren, pastor, a name to note), and past a well-kept cemetery, before crossing the Nodaway River on a rickety bridge and returning to the corn.

The left arm of the T zips past the B&B Grocery, a modern little store with supermarket aspirations (Ernest and Lois Bowenkamp, proprietors, also names to note). The grocery store is next door to the bank and directly across the street from the Sam R. Albright Post 48 American Legion Hall. There are a couple more little stores before this road too falls away over the roll, through another short stretch of unassuming homes, tailing away to another bridge across the Nodaway River again and reentering the corn.

Out there on the far bank of the Nodaway River, Skidmore, really so close by, is as far away as the buffalo.

*

Out there on the riverbank might be a good place to try to gather some perspective on Judgment Day, 1981. On the question of what it might have meant. It's the perfect place to ponder the mystery.

Two hundred years earlier, in 1781, newborn America, pinched up against the East Coast, learned that Daniel Boone (himself contemptuous of the society that spawned him and in his last days a legend and a Missourian) had opened a gateway through the Cumberland Gap to the West. The first great wave of settlers who poured in through that gate were coarse, unlettered, would-be farmers of English and Scotch-Irish descent, with names like Lincoln and Jackson, McCoy and McGee—and McElroy.

The land was for the taking, and the settlers, those

THE ROAD TO SKIDMORE

Europeans who streamed in by the millions, had no time or patience for the Indians, who held a different kind of claim to the land. The Europeans soon overpowered the Indians, both by force and by force of will. There was an ancestral foreshadowing here of Ken Rex McElroy and the manner in which he staked his claims.

At that time, the ancient Nodaway Empire lay lightly on this far corner of Missouri. Two Indian tribes—the Sac and the Fox—occupied these fertile saucers along the Nodaway River in the lowlands at the edge of the Great Plains. The tribes intermingled peacefully and the distinctions between them were lost on the white historians, who would later note their existence and call them Sac-Fox.

Here where the virgin hardwood forests of the East commingled with the savannah grass of the virgin prairie, the Sac-Fox camped along the glacial rolls, following the wild game that abounded, fishing in the clear streams, planting their corn. They lived and died, warred and worshiped, played lacrosse and doubleball, performed exotic tribal rituals.

The Sac-Fox were among the truly mystical tribes of the plains, with secret fraternal orders—called Metawiwini, Sisakyaweni, Wapanowiweni, and NanaKawinatawinoni—whose enchanting rites and bitter potions were said to give them magical powers. They could plunge their arms into boiling water without injury, pick up and hold hot coals, conjure balls of fire out of the air, and levitate stones and make them wheel and dance.

Legends, surely. But legends can motivate a people and stir them to group actions that defy and bewilder the outsiders and factfinders. There was a legend at work in Skidmore in the summer of 1981 too. What motivated Skidmore was not what it knew about Ken Rex McElroy but what it imagined. And not the few facts about his background and his activities, but the provocative tales those facts had engendered—tales that grew more lurid and irresistible with every retelling, until they finally subsumed those meager facts and created their own truth: a legend, and a compelling one.

The Sac-Fox people didn't know that they were wards of a succession of French and Spanish monarchs, of Napoleon, finally of the upstart Americans. Those absentee landlords hadn't disturbed them, and without alarm the Sac-Fox watched Lewis and Clark struggle up the nearby Missouri River, mapping the way for the coming horde. The doom of their fragile empire wasn't sealed until 1831, exactly fifty years after Daniel Boone opened the door to the West to the Lincolns and Jacksons, the McCoys and McElroys.

The "signing" of a treaty up in the Wisconsin territory in 1831 at an outpost named Prairie du Chien was the first of a fast succession of land grabs giving ownership of vast areas of the Midwest to the white men. It was a death warrant for a patchwork of Indian nations, including the Sac-Fox. Among the parties to it were chiefs whose proud names belied their humiliation—White Cloud, No Heart, Pumpkin, Hair Shedder, and One That Eats Rats.

One name was conspicuously missing: Black Hawk, the emperor whose domain stretched as far down as the Nodaway and whose people included the Sac and the Fox.

Black Hawk took up arms against this iron invasion, this outrageous system of justice that roosted in courthouses. (Black Hawk's first tragic act of defiance was actually crossing over into the land that had been taken from him and planting corn there.) The result was what historian

THE ROAD TO SKIDMORE

Marquis James called "a detail of Indian swindling which history obscures behind the respectable name of the Black Hawk War."

Calling it a "war" gave a chance to distinguish themselves to some of the politically ambitious young men whose grubby fathers had poured through the open door. Among those young men taking advantage of the war to further their careers were Abraham Lincoln, Zachary Taylor, William Henry Harrison, and Jefferson Davis. Within a year's time the force they served had annihilated Black Hawk's Stone Age warriors and massacred most of the tribal remnants.

Black Hawk himself was spared so he could be dragged, in ball and chains, before the treaty council at Prairie du Chien, there to be cajoled, ridiculed, and finally forced into signing away the empire he had tried to defend. Later he was taken to Washington, D.C., and presented as a sort of war prize to President Andrew Jackson, whose public policy toward Indians was simple genocide, and then paraded around the metropolises of the East like a side-show freak. After his death, his skeleton became a conversation piece when it was put on display in the office of an early governor of Iowa.

There were two conflicting views of Black Hawk back then. One saw him as a heroic martyr, and the other as a bullheaded troublemaker who finally got what he deserved. According to the latter view, he was a renegade, an outlaw, a disruptive force that a civilized society based on law and order simply couldn't tolerate. Or, as the survivors among his people might have said:

"The reason they all hated him was because he was a better man than any of them . . . he stood up for his rights and he wouldn't kneel down to them."

JUDGMENT DAY

A similar conflict, expressed in exactly the same terms, would beset Skidmore 150 years after the Treaty of Prairie du Chien. Skidmore described Ken Rex McElroy as an outlaw, a renegade, an intolerable disruptive force. And the words in the quotation above actually were spoken by Ken Rex's widow at a press conference a few days after his death.

The town of Skidmore was incorporated in 1881, a hundred years after Boone opened the door to the West, fifty years after the first Treaty of Prairie du Chien. By then practically all traces of Indian life, even of pioneer life, had disappeared from these glacial rolls, and, in fact, the settlement of Skidmore was not greatly different then from what it is today.

The population numbered about four hundred, then as now; the community interests and concerns were much the same. Already Skidmore was a settled, slow-paced little farming town nurtured by the flourishing agriculture in those surrounding saucers, which were already sweet with corn and sour with hogs.

One of the concerns, then as now, was crime. That was the famous Outlaw Era—the period of bank robberies, train robberies, and widespread cattle rustling, which the movies would later glamorize. The courthouse system of justice hadn't yet fully stabilized, and the result was that communities often took the law into their own hands and executed their own brand of swift justice.

Vigilantes lynched suspected rustlers by the dozen in Nebraska, just across the river. A mounted fraternity of night riders called the Bald Knobbers, in eared black hoods that gave them the look of jackals or demons, terrorized local troublemakers just downstate in southwest Missouri. Jesse James was killed—shot in the back—down at St. Joe just a few months after Skidmore's founding, and it wasn't uncommon for a "known character" in these parts to take a slug in the back in a crowded barroom and for witnesses to say they never saw a thing.

So "frontier justice" was a part of Skidmore's birthright. But if it was practiced early on in the Nodaway Empire, it was done with quiet efficiency so that it escaped official notice. Not until another fifty years, over at Maryville in 1931, did it erupt again into public view.

That was the case involving Raymond Gunn, a black man—one of the rare ones in these parts—the case in which Sheriff Harve England said he expected no mob violence but was prepared to call out the National Guard if need be. In fact, the governor of Missouri did send a detachment of National Guardsmen to Maryville to protect Raymond Gunn, but those guardsmen and the other authorities merely stood by while the mob did what it did.

What it did was this: It broke into the county jail, dragged Gunn across town to the schoolhouse where he was supposed to have raped and murdered a white teacher, lifted him up to the roof of the building, and there nailed him down, poured gasoline over his body, and burned him alive.

Another fifty-year jump to the summer of 1981 and sleepy little Skidmore delivered itself of Ken Rex McElroy, an "outlaw," a "troublemaker," a "known character," in what was sensationally reported across the country and around the world as another eruption of frontier justice. Ken Rex was shot from behind, in broad daylight, in front of a barroom, and scores of witnesses somehow never saw a thing.

JUDGMENT DAY

A vigilante killing?

"No way," said county prosecutor David Baird.

"Pure bunk," said Nodaway County Sheriff Danny Estes.

"No, not at all," said Jim Taylor, the Maryville newspaper reporter who brought the incident to national attention.

Skidmore itself is mute.

But this much is sure: Even if it was something less than a vigilante murder, it was also something more.

There was a brief, terrible drama here, and, because of the factual and moral confusion surrounding it, that drama has the proportions to become a modern myth.

Like all great myths, it can be read in different ways by different people—or even by the same person. It can be a tale of hope or a tale of doom. It can stir admiration or contempt or horror. And it has.

People everywhere who have ever been bullied or harassed or terrorized have put themselves, through their imaginations, at the scene there on the dusty street in Skidmore on the morning of July 10, 1981, and have asked themselves: What would I have done?

And the thoughtful ones go beyond that to the bigger and meaner question: What does it mean?

Driving back through Skidmore, you see a cluster of old men, most of them retired farmers, sitting on the bench in front of the American Legion Hall. A couple of them wave to whoever passes by. Though it's a warm day, they are wearing long-sleeved shirts and bib overalls. Two of them have on baseball caps, the others wide-brimmed straw hats. They sit talking idly about the corn crop or the price of hogs, about the prospects for this year's Punkin Festival, maybe even about the murder. Even that will enter the relaxed everyday conversation here sooner or later, if it hasn't already.

Ernest Bowenkamp, the septuagenarian grocer who was a principal in the prologue to the tragedy, is sitting there among those old farmers, looking not at all out of place.

If one were to turn again at the T, whisk by the bank, and impulsively wheel in and park in front of D&G's, one would be following the same route Ken Rex must have taken into town on Judgment Day, and perhaps even parking in the spot where he parked. Actually, thinking about this helps the mind's eye to see again all the events of that July morning:

A brown late-model Chevy pickup turns the corner up at the T, revs a time or two for show, then whips into the parking space with a flamboyant screech. A robust man, not tall but seeming to be, gets out and lumbers heavily toward the front door of the tavern. It is a hot day, and he is already sweating through his shirt. His arms look huge, and his body is stout with an overall puffiness that comes with drinking and age.

His wife, an attractive blonde and much younger than he, gets out the opposite pickup door and scuttles along in his wake. He goes into the tavern ahead of her, but she catches up to him when he hesitates just inside the door to survey the place with a practiced sweeping glance. He never enters a place without sizing it up with that glance, and he can read a situation with that glance better than a gambler can assay the slightest facial expression of an opponent at the poker table.

Outside, someone is hurrying along the street toward the big meeting that is in progress at the American Legion Hall around the corner. A lot of people are in town today. Something's in the air.

It's not long before the men come. They are not walk-

43

ing fast, but they're not ambling either. There is a certain deliberateness in their approach, an air of preoccupation that keeps them quiet. A hint of apprehension, almost hesitancy, at the edges of the shapeless group is compensated for by a kind of bravado that wells up from the middle.

The first ones duck quickly into the tavern—not pausing to think about it. The last ranks grow a little nervous as they wait to squeeze through. One or two of them hesitate a moment too long and at the last instant turn and walk quickly away back up the street and out of sight.

When they are all inside, Skidmore, for a few moments that seem many, goes as quiet as a ghost town. The tacky front of D&G's tells nothing. A mockingbird purls somewhere down around the Methodist church. An old couple in a pickup put-puts by, somehow unobtrusively, and the old man's face is as gaunt and expressionless as the moon's.

There is movement across the street near the crumbling step with the grass growing through it, but no one has noticed because all attention is on the tavern, and everyone wants to wedge through the door to see if this tense struggle that's been building for so long is being won or lost.

Then come the muffled voices rising inside the tavern, full of a mock-hearty camaraderie, perhaps just a little too loud to be convincing. It isn't long—it isn't long at all—before the door opens again. The puffy man comes out once more, this time with his left arm around his wife, who is walking close beside him. He is carrying a six-pack of cold beer, dangling it carelessly in his right hand.

At close range the features are pretty intimidating—the heavy jowls, the full Roman nose, the strong mouth and

black eyebrows, the thick dark hair and neat long side-
burns. And the eyes, deep-set and narrowed now against
the July dazzle—so penetrating that they strike zero at the
bone.

It is here that it stops, frozen at the bone. Those eyes,
narrowed against the sun or against something else, are all
that's left as he swings around the front of the pickup and
climbs heavily into the cab while his wife scrambles in on
the other side. The eyes are all that's left and they tell
nothing.

The men start coming out of the tavern to stand watching him, and now is when it all begins to spin away again,
disappearing into the maelstrom of myth, and when the
old familiar, comforting detachment resumes. Now would
be the only time still remaining to get inside the cab of the
pickup with him and ask him:

Why?

What was it you were always pushing to prove?

How far back did it go and how much longer would it
have gone on?

How much of the legend is true?

What was it that brought you to town this morning? Did
you come for a showdown with Skidmore or a showdown
with something more, something fated?

Did you *know*?

But the eyes tell nothing as he sits waiting, his thumb
and forefinger on the ignition key, waiting.

Then it all spins away.

The rest is myth.

Profile of a Legend

The heavy voice carried all the way down to the hayfield and all at once the boys were off the wagon and running. "Cow's having her calf!" one of the older boys yipped, but they already knew. They made a race of it up to the barn, their young voices breaking the quiet of the late summer day.

The youngest boy ran behind, trying to keep up, liking the run but feeling a dread inside. The heavy voice called again, impatient now. Beneath that came the low, alien moan of the cow in its agony.

The other boys reached the barn and stopped quickly just outside. The youngest one came up last, straggling a few yards away. "Come on, Kenny." He held back a little as the others went in.

The bitter smell of the place made them all stop suddenly. The man was moving urgently, his breath heaving. The cow kept up its excruciating plea as he knelt and tried to free it from the birthing pain.

The boys edged close finally, their eyes bright with fascination. "Come on, Kenny," one of them called again in a whisper. The small boy cringed. He wanted to stay back in the shadows, enough to say he was there with them, but what froze him was the terrible noise and the odor that stung his senses.

Suddenly the man stood up, his whole body trembling with urgency. He seemed to look past the boys as the cow bellowed louder. The time was critical—it was more than that, it was crucial if the animal was to be saved.

"Come here and help!" he barked out and pointed. His eyes swung directly toward the youngest boy there, as if he were choosing frantically at random. "Come here, Kenny!"

The other boys started to speak but quickly stopped, for they were a little afraid of it themselves. The youngest did not move.

"I said come here and help!"

Still the boy made no move to obey. The father took an angry stride and, jerking the boy up, pulled him back to the stall. Now the boy could see the cow's agony and the rupture of the breached, halfborn thing in front of him. He was caught, paralyzed by the odor that blinded his eyes.

His father knelt and made him take hold. "Now pull! Pull! Not like that! Pull harder!"

He fought against the fear welling inside him. His father's heavy breath was more a punishment than the animal's retching. He let his hands take hold and stay there; he fought back tears with all his might.

"Can't you do nothing? Pull, I said!"

Seconds later he felt himself falling away. He didn't know if his father had struck him or just pushed him. All he knew was that he was free of it. He sprawled to one side, his face covered by the stall's shadow. He couldn't hear his father's frantic heaving, couldn't hear him saying what he always said, that he was a sissy, a mamma's boy, a crybaby who wouldn't ever be a man.

He lifted his head and looked once. Now he couldn't even smell the stench that had killed his senses; he couldn't see the awful scene. He seemed to stare over it, beyond it all, past the humiliation into something he couldn't name. Maybe it was something akin to the animal's torment that broke inside him and gave way to anger and hatred. He didn't recoil at the sight as he stared on, and he knew he would never cringe or whimper again.

"Tony was real mean to that boy," old-time acquaintances from the Quitman years say. "He wasn't too good to the other kids either, but he seemed to have it in for Kenny."

Ken Rex was the twelfth of thirteen children born to Tony and Mabel McElroy at Quitman, a farming settlement of no more than fifty people, then and now, five miles north of Skidmore. Ken Rex could easily have become lost in the shuffle of all those brothers and sisters, but that wasn't to be his lot. His father, Tony, singled out Ken Rex early.

Maybe the times had something to do with that. All Tony McElroy needed in the summer of 1934, with eleven children already, was another mouth to feed. It was the worst time in American history to be a farmer. In the Midwest, dust storms whirled up by prolonged droughts smothered the parched cornfields. Corn that didn't burn up in the fields wouldn't sell after the harvest; its only value was as feed for hogs, and the hogs wouldn't sell either. The government finally began to pay farmers to shoot the hogs just to get rid of them.

JUDGMENT DAY

The despair of the farmers—especially the poorest ones with great broods of hungry children looking at them expectantly—took many forms of expression, and one of the milder ones was an impotent and irrational lashing out at whoever happened to be handy. Often, maybe out of guilt, the farmers' anger was directed at the most vulnerable of those around them, at the new mouth there, unasked for, clamoring to be fed.

The grinding poverty of the Depression seems to have brought out both the best and the worst in Tony McElroy. He and his wife got by somehow, got all the kids raised, and that was no small accomplishment. But it took everything Tony McElroy had for him to break even with the world. He never got a chance to really be somebody.

Born before the turn of the century, he had come from a poor rural background, had received no schooling, had married early, and started breeding right away. Now it seemed his destiny to be worn down and worn out by the brutal Depression, scratching out a mean living on a little farm at Quitman in a forgotten niche of the Nodaway Empire.

Like most men, Tony wanted to be somebody whom his neighbors and the world could take notice of. Like the McElroy down in Kansas City who was a kingpin in the Pendergast political machine. But as the years passed and the kids kept coming and the toil got harder and less rewarding, nobody cared about Tony McElroy. So he compensated by becoming a blowhard.

If he couldn't *be* somebody, he could at least talk like a somebody. He did just that, regaling the leisurely Saturday-afternoon gatherings at country stores and sale barns around Nodaway County with bluster about how tough he was. He was a stout and bullish man, as Ken Rex would grow up to be, and he talked a mean game about what he could and would do to anyone foolish enough to mess with him. His bombast didn't impress his neighbors, but it probably did impress his little boy Ken Rex, who could not have known that it was all just empty talk. The boy would have thought there were deeds behind those daring words. His father had unwittingly given Ken Rex a role model.

Old stories exist around Nodaway County about how Tony McElroy took young Ken Rex with him to the stores in Skidmore and the auction barns at Maryville. He would use the boy in his attempts to draw attention to his own imagined machismo—would make fun of Ken Rex in front of the older men by portraying the child as a sissy and a mamma's boy in contrast to his own two-fisted manner. Even if he did it out of thoughtlessness rather than cruelty, it humiliated the boy in a way that he never got over. It set up a conflict in Ken Rex that he would try with increasing desperation for the next forty years to resolve.

Ken Rex fared poorly in school. He wasn't much interested in book learning because he had something to prove—not only that he was not the sissy his father held him up to be, but also that he was somebody who was going to gain the attention and respect of everybody around him. In the only way he knew how—his father's way. It didn't take Ken Rex long to get the name of a classroom troublemaker.

It was the custom in the rural schools of the time for teachers to separate such problem children from the others, to ignore them as much as possible, and to use them as negative examples for the other children. Then, also, the teachers passed their problem students along from one grade to the next simply to get rid of them. That is why it was entirely possible for such children to go through several years of school without ever learning how to read and write.

A troubled and troublesome boy like Ken Rex had to go to great lengths to assert himself, to prove that in his isolation he was not inferior but actually superior. He was able to put on a convincing show in that regard because his physical development was rapid. Even before he dropped out of school in the sixth grade he was regarded as something of a terror not only by his classmates but also by his teachers. As he grew older, he began to miss more school than he attended, but his teachers—whose pet name for him was "dummy"—kept passing him along.

Like his father, Ken Rex had barely learned to write his name when he dropped out of school around the age of eleven. But he had learned some things about human relations, even though they were all the wrong things. He would, in his later years, speak arrogantly about his lack of education. He couldn't escape the fact of his functional illiteracy, which must have whispered the dreaded word "inferiority" in the back of his mind, but he could mask the feeling or compensate for it by flashing big wads of money in the taverns and telling his drinking buddies: "Look at that, would you? I got more of it at home too, a whole damn trunkful. Not bad for a man who can't even read and write."

Conspicuous money gave the lie to those whisperings of inferiority, and that fact probably accounts for Ken Rex's becoming the provincial champion at a kind of money game that's a tradition in the bars of the region. It's a game that two beer drinkers use to decide who has to buy the next round:

The first man slaps a dollar down on the bar. The second man covers it with a dollar of his own. First man then slaps down a five, and the second man covers that. They work up through twenties, fifties, hundreds. The first one to run out of money loses the game. It's a pretty common sight to see men stacking up four or five thousand dollars just to see who'll buy a sixty-cent beer. Ken Rex loved to play the game and he never lost.

The attraction-repulsion relationship between Ken Rex and his father got more tense as Ken Rex grew up. The incident of the cow giving birth to its calf is most revealing of this tension. The boy was frightened over the incident, as a child would be, but the incident reveals more—that Ken Rex's shrewd, distorted way of looking at every challenge was already keenly developed. In his view, his father was testing him, putting him in an intolerable position in front of his brothers, the same way he had held him up to scorn before those old men around the sale barns.

Maybe his father really did need his help for a minute, but Ken Rex's mind was already turned in that peculiar direction so that he could not have seen the incident in such simple terms. Tony McElroy told the story around afterward, using it to illustrate his own toughness and his little boy's lack of it.

Not long after the episode, Ken Rex made a vow to his companions that he wasn't going to put up with his father's bullying much longer. He then said something he was to say often before he was grown and after: "You kick a dog long enough, it's going to bite you."

That was a prophecy. As it turned out, it was a two-edged one.

When Ken Rex was almost eleven he got hurt. He was big for his age, already strong enough for his father to put him to work as a field hand. One day Ken Rex and his brothers were hauling hay and Ken Rex was riding atop a load as the wagon was coming to the barn from the meadow. When one of the wagon's wheels hit a chuckhole, the load shifted, pitching the boy forward and dropping him headfirst to the ground.

He was knocked unconscious. His family got him to the hospital in Maryville, where he lay in a semicoma for many hours. Fearing brain damage, the doctors arranged to transfer him to a larger hospital at St. Joseph. There he began to make a slow recovery.

Some of the news stories after his death contended that doctors at St. Joseph had put a metal plate in his skull, but that turned out to be untrue. The coroner's report and the autopsy confirmed that there had been no metal plate in Ken Rex's head. Furthermore, there are no medical records of his having any kind of surgical operations during his childhood.

It is a fact, however, that Ken Rex fell from a haywagon and sustained a serious injury. Some people in Skidmore have said that the injury changed him. Afterward, he became subject to violent temperamental outbursts, they say, and there was a willfulness and an intensity to his mischief that had never been there before. Of course, the change in him might have been the result of pressures that had nothing to do with brain damage. He was entering adolescence, and that could have had an incendiary effect on a personality that had been warped early on. And he was getting big enough and old enough to start making good on the rebellious vow he had made to his companions.

He suffered another serious head injury when he was eighteen. He was a part-time construction worker at the time and his crew was on a job near St. Joe, when a steel slab fell and hit him in the head. He was hospitalized again, and this injury, too, has been cited as a possible explanation for some of his later depredations.

There's no way to know. Until the time of his death, Ken Rex did occasionally exhibit strange physical symptoms that could have been attributable to neurological damage, which in turn caused his erratic behavior. One of those symptoms was frequent, copious nosebleeds, which sometimes were so severe that he had to be hospitalized. One of his hunting buddies has described another symptom. They would be out hunting, he said, just walking along, when Ken Rex would suddenly collapse. He would be out cold for a minute, then he would come around, get up, and go on as if nothing had happened. When his buddy tried to help or to offer to take him to a doctor, Ken Rex would brush the whole thing off, pretend it had never happened, and say, "Ain't nothing wrong with me. Nothing at all."

Even if these episodes came from nothing more dramatic than his chronic high blood pressure, they somehow made the legend of Ken Rex scarier. They made people imagine that he was not just mean, but also unbalanced— that while there was method in his calculating madness, there was also a clinically traceable strain of derangement that made him unpredictable and therefore a much greater threat to the community at large. Psychos scare us all in a way that mere thugs don't.

Ken Rex did develop one admirable trait as a boy, and that was a love of animals. His particular fondness for hunting dogs would become one of the main interests in his life

JUDGMENT DAY

Tony McElroy was never so poor that he didn't keep at least one bony old coon hound around the place, and he usually kept several. As a boy, Ken Rex became attached to those dogs; he discovered that he had a gift for training them. His father took him to some of the Saturday-night coon dog field trials—a major entertainment in little towns around Nodaway County. Ken Rex picked up a knowledge of training techniques, and by the time he was a teen-ager he was winning some of the field competitions.

He soon got a reputation as the best coon dog trainer in Nodaway County, a distinction grudgingly awarded because coon hound training is a passion with hunters, and it seemed to come too easily to Ken Rex. With some remarkable intuition he possessed, Ken Rex seemed able to inspire his dogs, especially those that showed little ability or promise to start with.

"He had the knack of taking any fair dog and making it a whole lot better," one of his hunter friends said. "Without question, he was the best trainer around. Everybody knew it."

After the construction-site accident, Ken Rex gave up any notion of working at a regular job. He found that dealing in hogs and dogs was safer and more profitable. Later on, he would make a little legitimate money by dealing in antiques and leasing out some of the land he had inherited from his father, but his coon dogs were his main legal pursuit.

He belonged to the Nodaway County coon dog association, and about the only people he would ever be able to call friends were fellow coon hunters. His reputation as a trainer grew, to the point that dog owners from all over were coming to him for training tips, and also to buy or trade dogs. Buying was serious business, since a good dog in those parts might sell for as much as three or four thousand dollars. In this small and exclusive fraternity, Ken Rex got to be a somebody in a way that his father never did. He was not only proving himself to the old man, but also pacifying the demon inside himself. He was enough of a somebody so that later his hunting buddies would refuse to believe he had been the terror that the rest of the world portrayed him as being.

Because of his reputation as a trainer, few others would challenge him in the field trials. So he worked up a little scheme—a kind of coon dog sting—which allowed him to continue proving his superiority as a trainer. It also brought him nice sums of money.

This is how the scam worked. Let's say a field trial would be coming up in an out-of-the-way place, over in another county or up in Iowa. Ken Rex would deliver one of his hounds, a proven winner, to one of his hunting pals, who in turn would enter the dog in the trials as an untested novice. A main event in field trials is a contest to determine which dog can tree a raccoon the fastest and bay it the longest. During these events the dog owners indulge in substantial wagering and side-betting. Often, Ken Rex's buddy would return from one of these contests with hundreds and even thousands of dollars, which he and Ken Rex would then split fifty-fifty.

By the early 1950s, with most of the children married and gone, the McElroys had taken up residence on a scruffy farm a few miles south of Skidmore. Ken Rex was coming of age and creating his tough image. The hard-working people of Skidmore disapproved of this over-grown, mean-looking boy who ambled the streets of their town as if he owned them. He wore tight T-shirts with the sleeves cut out to reveal his huge biceps. And he developed a habit of staring malevolently at people in a way that unnerved many of them. He had no regular job and no inclination to work at all, yet he roared around the countryside in a new Buick convertible and flashed big wads of money.

It also grated on Skidmore that he already had the name of a lady-killer. Although he married young, as his father had, and wasted no time siring offspring, Ken Rex made few concessions to the conventional sexual morality of rural Nodaway County. Sex and violence were the stuff his legend was made of, and it was the sex that stirred people's outrage the most in those early years and that generated the most fear.

In the beginning, Ken Rex seems to have used sex in the way most young toughs used it. Sex and cars and fighting were the three ways that studs competed for recognition and dominance, as they still do today in most places. But most young men grow up, settle for what they can get, and make a place for themselves in the scheme of things.

Not Ken Rex.

Because of his insatiable need to prove himself, Ken Rex kept on carousing even as he went through several marriages, legal or otherwise. His sexual approach was simple and brazen: When he saw a girl he wanted, he went after her. And he kept after her until he got her, one way or the other. His sharp intuitive sense always told him which ones he could pursue successfully, and his obsessive drive to prove himself meant trouble for anyone who got in the way—parents, boyfriends, or husbands.

Ken Rex's greatest conquest—and the one that earned him the most notoriety—was that of Trena McCloud. It happened in the early 1970s, when Ken Rex was already pushing forty and Trena barely in her teens. Ken Rex's first wife had left after bearing him five children and, although it's uncertain that he was ever legally divorced, he was living as man and wife with Alice Woods, whisking her away from her home when she was fifteen years old. He was also said to have established a far-flung and informal harem—lonely women scattered from northern Kansas to eastern Nebraska to southern Iowa, with much of northwest Missouri thrown in for seasoning. These women served him, among other ways, as fences for rustled livestock and stolen merchandise that he was said to be trafficking in.

Despite the impressive testimonial to his sexual prowess that these women represented, Ken Rex wanted little Trena.

Trena was a pretty girl, a comely blonde with a woman's figure even in early adolescence. She was a neighbor's child, and Ken Rex had had his eye on her a long time. It is possible originally he was interested in her mother, but that as the little girl began to flower, his attention gravitated more and more her way.

Trena's school friends remember that Ken Rex haunted the school yard, waiting for her to get out of class, and that she would point him out and say, "That's my boyfriend." Sometimes he would wait for the school bus a short ways out of town. He would sit there in his pickup, not moving a muscle and not seeming to notice anyone on the bus, which gave the kids an eerie feeling. Trena would get off the bus and go with him—not necessarily homeward.

After Trena got involved with Ken Rex, she became a problem to her parents and the authorities, according to former Nodaway County Sheriff John Middleton. Her parents didn't want Ken Rex hanging around, but he was too forceful to keep away. The situation became so critical that the county authorities stepped in and took Trena away, placing her in a foster home. That did little good either.

John Middleton, the one who went out and got Trena and took her to the foster home, recalled those days.

"Ken Rex drove those people crazy," Middleton said. "He wouldn't leave Trena alone. He went to her foster parents and made threats, and they'd come to me and say they couldn't keep her any longer. The court would find her another home. The same thing happened three or four times, until nobody would keep her."

Meanwhile Trena's mother had remarried, and the girl's stepfather decided to stand up to Ken Rex. He went to the courthouse and filed a rape charge. Soon thereafter, his house near Skidmore burned to the ground. The step-father, too, had had enough then. He and Trena's mother fled the state, leaving behind their other belongings, including Trena.

Ken Rex was charged not only with rape, but also with arson. When he showed up in court, the arson charge was dropped for failure of witnesses to appear. And the rape charge had to be dropped too—not because Trena wasn't there to testify, but because she and Ken Rex had found a judge in another state to marry them. Spouses can't testify against each other in Missouri.

In the wave of publicity following Ken Rex's death, Trena denied that Ken Rex had ever raped her. She said the fire which sent her folks packing was caused by faulty wiring. She staunchly defended Ken Rex against all criticism. So did Alice Woods, who had shared her bedroom

60

with Trena after Ken Rex brought her home. Alice stayed on to help with the children—she and Trena each contributing three, and there being four besides from Ken Rex's first marriage still at home.

If Ken Rex was capable of love, then Trena must have been the true love of his life. He went to a lot of trouble to get her, pushing his luck as never before and coming close to having to stand trial for rape and arson. Right up to the end, the two of them seemed to have a special closeness that one sees only in well-matched lovers. They went all places together and looked like they belonged together.

Skidmore didn't seem to doubt the genuineness of Trena's grief when he died, even if it snorted at her portrayal of him as an all-American husband and father who had been much maligned and misunderstood. Maybe the Ken Rex–Trena affair was a tragic, touching love story. But in the end, with the coming of Judgment Day, it didn't matter if Ken Rex had really loved Trena or if he had merely brutalized her into submission. It didn't matter if he had raped and ruined her or had lovingly brought her into womanhood, honestly cherishing her as a kind of idealized image of what he perceived as the sweet, anguished, vulnerable side of himself that he had hidden so well for so long.

Nor did it matter, in the context of that larger tragedy, how much truth there was in such widely circulated rumors as these:

—One time Ken Rex ambled into a saloon in St. Joe with one of his women on one arm and a long roll of bologna under the other. He had been drinking heavily, so he was louder than usual. He banged on the bar and made this announcement:

"I'm gonna take this bitch to the motel and I'm gonna

61

screw her with this stick of baloney and find out just how much she can take. I'll lay odds, if any of you sumbitches are interested."

—One night one of Ken Rex's women turned up at the emergency room of the Maryville hospital. She was crying hysterically and the front of her blouse was soaked with blood. When the attendants removed her clothing, they found that a nipple was missing from one of her breasts. Ken Rex, they were told, had got carried away. He had bitten the nipple off.

—There was another little farm girl. And another war of wills between Ken Rex and the girl's parents. Another triumph and another conquest. Only this time the girl was so emotionally traumatized that she wound up in the state mental hospital, where she is still a patient.

—And then, just a year before Judgment Day, Ken Rex shot Ernest Bowenkamp, the Skidmore grocer, and Pastor Tim Warren of the Skidmore Christian church visited Bowenkamp in the hospital. Soon after the pastor returned to the parsonage in Skidmore, the telephone rang and a husky voice offered a warning:

"Keep your sympathy for old man Bowenkamp to yourself, preacher, or your wife will be getting a package in the mail and one of her tits will be inside."

In the end it didn't matter how much of all this was true. All that mattered was that such facts, fancies, half-truths, and apocryphal tales created an image of Ken Rex as a sexual predator, almost a sexual monster—one who scorned all the sexual conventions and spurned the laws regarding acceptable sexual conduct.

The rapist is still the most reviled and despicable of criminals in the minds of most Americans, more so even than the murderer. Unlike the murderer, the rapist isn't a rare threat who comes up suddenly and then is gone. The rapist is always out there, surreptitious and unfathomable, threatening unrelentingly to violate and plunder. It is a crucial part of the legend of Ken Rex McElroy that Skidmore considered him a rapist who would go after little girls if they struck his fancy; a rapist to whom vile sexual acts and terroristic mutilation were not unthinkable.

In an indirect way, some of Ken Rex's most loyal defenders reinforced the image of him as a sexual predator in their tributes to him after his murder.

One of his wives was quoted as saying: "People didn't like him because their wives chased him. And he was partly to blame for it, because he didn't run when they chased him."

And this from one of his brothers: "Girls were crazy about him. The men didn't like that. Of course, you're not going to hear that in Skidmore. People aren't going to say they can't hold their wives."

That, too, amounts to a view of Ken Rex as a sexual threat to the community. And it echoes Skidmore's view, yet in a vastly different way. It is like the similarity and radical difference between lovemaking and rape, between a sexual fantasy and a sexual nightmare.

Ken Rex once said he had his first brush with the law when he was thirteen years old. Like so many of his brushes with the law, that incident didn't get into the record. One published account contends that he was caught stealing by a neighboring farm wife and threatened to burn down her house if she reported him. Whatever the details, the odds are that the incident did involve stealing.

Ken Rex was never in his life convicted of stealing anything. One of his wives stated vehemently after his death that she had never known him to steal anything. But Skidmore believed that as much as it believed Trena's remark about the "faulty wiring" that caused her folks' house to burn down. At the time of his death, Ken Rex had the reputation in Skidmore of being the most accomplished thief to come out of the area since Jesse James. If any part of his legend is secure, it is the part that portrays him as a kind of Jesse James of the hog lots, as daring in his way as Jesse was, and finally killed the same way—shot from the back.

"I've heard him called a small-time thief," says John Middleton, the former sheriff. "He wasn't a small-time thief. He was a *big*-time thief."

He probably got into stealing the same way he got into sex and cars and fighting. It was the next step up for the rural young tough out to make a name for himself. Stealing for the hell of it, just to show off—for the same basic reason that Tony McElroy had done all that big talking.

And without regard to the value of what was stolen—pumpkins or birdbaths or hubcaps or pieces of farm machinery left overnight in a cornfield—just to show that he could get away with it. To show people that he could rip them off and they couldn't do anything about it—if they knew what was good for them.

Here was a good one: snatching a big old hog gazing serenely through a fence beside the road. Anyone burly and bold enough to waltz right up there in the moonlight and grab a two-hundred-pound pig and flop him over into the backseat of his car and drive off into the night with him was already on his way to becoming a legend.

In one of Skidmore's vivid memories of Ken Rex, he is bopping along Skidmore's main drag early in the evening in his convertible, all dressed up and after-shaved for his womanizing, the car radio trailing strains of Elvis Presley—with a big old dazed-looking hog lolling in the backseat.

He was probably stealing more for the fun than for the profit of it at that time, although he was already flashing money around. Both the mood and the motive had changed by the time of the next story, which was also to work its way into the legend.

It is the story of a lone deputy sheriff sitting in his patrol car at a county crossroads late at night, lights off, waiting. He's out there because there have been more than the usual number of calls to the courthouse in recent nights about rustlers working in the vicinity.

The visor of his cap pulled low, the deputy sits scrunched behind the wheel, a little sleepy in the slow drag of the small hours of the night. But then the moonlit circular horizon fades as a slow glow moves up along the gravel road to the deputy's left. He leans forward over the wheel and squints hard at the approaching headlights. With a half-smile that quickly tenses, he says to himself, "By God, I got the bastard this time!"

The deputy starts the car and guns it forward, slinging gravel and raising dust, to block the road. He whips on the spotlight and whirls it to throw its beam directly on the approaching vehicle. He sees a brand-new Buick convertible.

The convertible stops dead in the road. The deputy gets out of the patrol car and approaches with a flashlight. The night is still and the dust he stirred up hangs heavily in the air, diffusing the flashlight's beam. The music blaring on the car radio in the convertible dies abruptly. In the stillness that follows, the deputy turns his light on the face of the car's driver. He starts to say something but stops short at the low, restive grunt of a pig. He hears a grunt, a snuffle, then a high-pitched squeal.

The deputy turns the flashlight toward the commotion and is startled to see, looking up at him from the backseat, one, then two, then three, then four half-grown shoats wriggling and squirming over one another.

"Jesus Christ," the deputy says.

"How's that?"

The voice from the front seat is a raspy, almost inaudible whisper.

The deputy turns the light back on the driver and says, "What are you doing out here with all these damn pigs?"

The driver looks at him impassively for a long moment before he replies, "They belong to me."

"Yeah? You want to tell me where you got 'em?"

Still with the same slow, measured indifference, the driver says, "I don't have to tell you shit."

"All right, buddy. You want to get out of that car?"

The driver says nothing, does not move. He rests his big forearms on the steering wheel and looks straight ahead through the windshield and the hanging dust into the glare of the spotlight and into the nothing beyond it.

The deputy hesitates. Quickly the driver's eyes dart and come back to a dead focus. He has seen the deputy's one little show of holding back, and that is all he needs to know.

"You know I can get on the radio in my car and have a backup unit here in two minutes," the deputy says.

"You don't want to do that."

"I don't, huh? You want to tell me why?"

"You just don't."

"Are you threatening me?"

No reply. Nothing.

The deputy hesitates again and shakes his head. He lets out a nervous little laugh. Still the man in the convertible has not budged, has not dropped his hard gaze straight ahead into the windshield. The deputy clenches his grip on the flashlight and assumes a stern tone.

"Look, I'm gonna let you go this time, punk. I ain't got nothing on you this time, but you damn sure better—"

"You want to move that car?"

"What?"

"And don't call me punk ever again."

"What'd you say?"

"I said move that goddamn car. These hogs are hell on my seat covers."

That was an early story showing how Ken Rex could read fear in people and understand how to exploit it. The one trait most often mentioned about him after his death was the way he could stare people down. What he was actually doing was measuring people, reading them the same way a doctor reads a medical chart or a stockbroker reads a market report. Put him in a courtroom, a bar, among a group of farmers, with a woman, and he would reveal a quiet intensity that struck people as menacing. He was sizing people up. He was assessing their fear, vulnerability, strength, courage. In short, he was determining what it would take to intimidate them and turn them to his strong will.

"If I decide to grab a few hogs off this man, what will it take to keep him from giving me any trouble? How much resistance will I get if I decide to have this woman? What's the weakness in this witness that I can work on to shut him up?"

JUDGMENT DAY

He wasn't one to ever let his guard down. He always knew where he stood with people he encountered, and the main reason he lasted as long as he did both as an outlaw and a stud was that he knew who to hit (and hit on) and who to leave alone. That was the gift he had—one that psychiatrists say is symptomatic of the psychopathic personality.

It was important to him, of course, to establish quickly and accurately how he stood with the various lawmen he came up against. He had no trouble with the irresolute deputy who caught him with those pigs, but sometimes the cold stare wasn't enough to give him a reliable reading of a man. There were a few lawmen over the years who were made of tough stuff, and Ken Rex knew instinctively not to mess with them. He never gave them any trouble—was even deferential in their presence. Some of these same officers remarked later, after Ken Rex's Judgment Day, that they really couldn't understand why people were so afraid of him.

"He was a pretty good old boy," according to them.

Without knowing it, these officers were paying tribute to Ken Rex's uncanny ability to read them right.

As Ken Rex got older and wiser, he became less flamboyant in his thievery. He had proven himself and was now a professional, content to make a good living at it. It's possible that even people close to him—his children, his brothers and sisters, certainly his aged mother—didn't know he was a big-time thief. Probably no one knew how *much* he stole. No one will ever know now.

And as he grew older, Ken Rex, like the Godfather, didn't like his family asking too many questions about his business. He didn't like *anybody* asking about it. When people he liked did ask, he usually laughed the questions away or gave them spiels about the investments he had in livestock farms scattered around the region, or about the good money he was making selling and trading antiques. People he didn't like knew better than to ask. Skidmore had no doubt that he had come to be as talented and unscrupulous at rustling as he was at training dogs.

And Ken Rex got shrewder. There's another story to illustrate this. A group of lawmen were closing in on him one night when he was driving his pickup down one of the country roads near Skidmore, pulling a whole trailer load of stolen cattle. One of the officers made the mistake of saying something over the police radio which alerted Ken Rex, listening in on his scanner, to the danger. So when Ken Rex approached a lone-lane bridge, he motioned his backup unit—that is, one of his women following in another pickup—to go on across the bridge ahead of him. Then he stopped his truck on the bridge, pulled it loose from the trailer, and left the load of livestock sitting on the bridge. He scrambled home and telephoned the sheriff's office to report that his cattle trailer had been stolen earlier that evening. He lost the stolen cows—temporarily, at least—but he got his trailer back, and he complimented the officers for their efficiency in recovering his property.

*

So as Ken Rex grew older and wiser, a ritual developed in the Nodaway Empire:

Night comes benignly to the rolling plains. From over the glacial roll, across the lapidary cornfields, rides the tinkling of cowbells. A farm woman, her apron still wet from the supper dishes, walks out on the front porch to call the children in and to catch the first cool breeze of the evening. From the tall sycamores, there comes the first skreak of the cicadas. The sky is the color of ink as dusk rises like smoke in the east.

There is a slow gathering of darkness as ownership of the earth passes to the night creatures and night forces.

At midnight the accumulated stillness opens for a moment to allow the passing of the lonely bugling of coon hounds somewhere down along the river bottom, and then it closes again. The estranging note of a solitary nighthawk ahunt over thick bean fields is a part of it. And so is the woolly worm's continued frantic, epic journey across the road.

Then the unheard choiring of a million bugs gives way suddenly to a heard silence. The sound begins a mile away—a dull drone that becomes the distinct sound of heavy tires flumping along the rough road. Headlights pitch up along the distant roll, then sink again into the deep of the cornfields.

Inside the house, a farmer is awakened by the heard silence; he leans to his bedroom window and peers out toward the disturbed starlight, which vanishes as the headlight beams slash the window and throw long shadows across the ceiling and down the wall. His wife stirs beside him and asks, "What is it?"

"Nothing. Crazy kids hot-rodding around likely."

But she knows better, for she picks up the heightened wariness in his voice and in his silhouette like a compass needle.

"Somebody's out there," she says.

The vehicle stops, engulfed by the trailing dust cloud. Heavy footsteps crunch across the yard without hurry and without stealth, heading toward the barn. The farmer feels under the bed for his gun. His wife reaches for the switch on the lamp, but he tells her, "Leave it off."

They hear, from down around the barn, the first snorts and bumpings of cattle being jostled. The farmer takes up the shotgun, letting the butt of it rest on the floor. He holds it absently with one hand on the barrel. He is trying to make up his mind.

The animal grunts louden and one of the cows lows mournfully. A loud curse, then a slap, then a long unguarded laugh, as though meant to be heard.

The farmer takes up the shotgun with both hands and holds it across his lap. He stirs as if to get up, but his wife puts a hand on his shoulder.

"Think of the kids—"

When it's all over, the headlights recede and the insect choir resumes. The man and woman sit for a long time in the same pose, saying nothing, each alone in a swarm of thoughts. The farmer won't go out and see what he already knows. Neither of them will sleep. They hold a vigil of silence as the small hours slip toward morning and dew awns the earth like the sheen of moth wings. They both hear the nighthawk, whose two-note chitter grates on the night like a jeer.

And then the morning.

Or a whole day of hesitation might pass before the futile interview:

"Did you actually see him stealing stock on your place?" the sheriff asks.

"Sure I did. I was right there by the window."

"So you can make a positive identification?"

"Well . . . I know it was him. I'd stake my life on it. You know how he operates, Sheriff."

"Yeah, I know how he operates. But I know how his

lawyer operates too. You can't go to court from looking out a window. Did you actually see him out there or not?"

"Nobody else operates that way. Come roaring up at two in the morning. Started loading up my stock like it belonged to him. And me knowing damn well what'd happen if I turned on the light, much less go out there. He wouldn't think no more about shooting up a man's house than he'd think of shooting up a tin can. Why can't you go down to his place and find my stock? My brand is on every one of 'em."

"Your stock won't be there. You know that. He ain't dumb. That stock is out of the county by now."

"Well, look, Sheriff. Here's a man with two women living with him and a pack of kids, plus all them high-priced coon dogs to feed. Driving brand-new pickups and flashing big rolls of money. Where's that money coming from if it ain't from rustling stock?"

"You tell me."

"Can't you go down there and make him answer?"

"I could *ask* him. I did ask him one time. Know what he told me? Told me he was a hit man for the North Kansas City mob. Didn't crack a smile when he said it."

"Couldn't you arrest him on that?"

"On what?"

"You mean it's not against the law to be a hired killer?"

"I can't arrest him for bragging. Even if I believed him, which I don't. His lawyer would laugh us out of court."

"Well, what about my stock?"

"If you'll sign me a complaint, saying you got reason to believe he stole some of your stock, I'll see what the prosecutor will do."

"Sign a complaint?"

"Will you do it or not?"

"You know what would happen if I was to do that. I'd start getting calls telling me I'd better back off. And then he'd make threats on my wife and kids. He'd be perched out there on a turnrow on the hood of his pickup with a shotgun. It happened to a friend of mine. You know about that. And I'd have to wonder if my house would burn down with all of us in it. He's set a fire or two before. He's done a lot worse than that."

"I'll try to get him," the sheriff says. "I'll try to see he don't bother you."

"You'll *try?*"

"I'll try. If I was to come out there and catch him sitting in a field with a gun, he'd just say he was shooting at some crows."

"Yeah, I guess so. Even if I ran him off myself, all I'd be thinking about would be my wife at the house by herself when I have to be gone. And the kids . . ."

"I'll do what I can. But I can't make it a twenty-four-hour job to watch somebody."

"That's not good enough, Sheriff."

"I know it's not. But this county's got eight hundred square miles in it. Got twenty thousand people and eighteen little towns and close to a thousand miles of road I have to cover. And I got two men to cover it with."

"I wouldn't get my stock back anyway, would I?"

"Not likely."

"I guess I'll just let it go then. But it ain't right."

"I wish I could do something, but my hands are tied. We'll catch the son of a bitch red-handed one of these days, I promise you."

"He's been caught red-handed before, ain't he? And nothing come of that either."

73

"All I can tell you, he gives you any more trouble, you just let me know."

"Like I done this time? God, I just hope he don't find out I come in here to see you."

With every such horror story spawning more like it—with all the cons, sexual forays, thefts, frights, and rumors—the legend of Ken Rex McElroy grew. It grew until he became the dark side of the moon whose bright side belonged to Dale Carnegie, the other Nodaway County native son. Both of them were celebrated manipulators of people, but one was the apostle of sunshine, the other the lord of the night. The title of Ken Rex's book would have been *How to Win Enemies and Influence People.*

Quicksand Years

Salus populi suprema lex esto. ("The welfare of the people shall be the supreme law.")

—Official motto of the state of Missouri

Following Ken Rex's death, prosecuting attorney David Baird of Maryville expressed his annoyance with newspaper references to Ken Rex's "long arrest record."

"Those reporters," Baird said, "are able to come up with only five arrests, and only one conviction, which I was able to get. Now to me, with all the riffraff I'm used to dealing with, *five* is not a long arrest record."

Only five arrests. If that meant to the prosecutor that Ken Rex was a negligible criminal compared to some of Nodaway County's "riffraff" with longer rap sheets, it meant something quite different to Skidmore.

To Skidmore it meant that Ken Rex was better at

75

breaking the law than the authorities were at enforcing it. Those five arrests (actually there could have been as many as fifty spread around a four-state area) involved two shootings, a rape, theft, terrorism, and burning down a family's home. The net result, aside from that one conviction, was that Ken Rex had to pay one fine of five hundred dollars. He never spent a night in jail—not an hour, not a single minute. The one conviction was for a crime so brutal that it shocked and enraged the whole community, and the conviction was on a reduced charge, so that the sentence, which Ken Rex didn't live to serve, was ridiculously lenient.

"Only five arrests." What that meant to Skidmore, in short, was that Ken Rex could commit just about any crime short of killing and not have to worry very much about the legal consequences.

Ken Rex had such a "feel" for his home territory—knowing what he could get away with in the Nodaway Empire, who he could push and who he couldn't—that he avoided serious trouble with the law until he was almost forty. Significantly, it wasn't the authorities of Nodaway County, but those of Buchanan County, down in St. Joe, who pinned the first felony charge on him.

That was early in 1972 and the charge stemmed from an incident in a St. Joe bar during which Ken Rex was supposed to have threatened to kill a man, first with a knife and later with a semiautomatic shotgun. He was charged and then set free on bond, and soon another felony charge was added to the first—for attempting to bribe a witness in the case. He wasn't on his home turf, and his tactics seemed to be getting him in deeper and deeper trouble.

A less intuitive criminal—one given to the cause-and-effect process of reasoning that most of us call good sense—might have backed off at that point, hoping that his lawyer was adept enough to undo some of the damage. Or he might have panicked and done something truly rash, something that would have landed him in the penitentiary for a long time.

But Ken Rex wasn't one to back off or to panic.

In sizing up his predicament, he surely reached back to his early years for guidance. He thought back to the time of the birth of the calf and realized that his mistake back then had been his failure to anticipate trouble. His thinking now would have been not to wait there in the barn shadows for his father to call him, but to set the barn on fire when the cow first went into labor. Similarly, these felony charges against him now demanded preventive action. If he waited around until the trial, someone else would settle the matter for him.

He might have thought back to other encounters. The one with that skittish deputy on the dark country road, for instance. He could have turned his pig-laden car around and tried to escape; he could have given up and trusted the resourcefulness of his lawyer to help him beat the rap. Or he could have physically assaulted the deputy. Instead, he intimidated the deputy almost wordlessly, using the deputy's own imagination against him, persuading him with nothing more than a tone of voice and a cold look that the final issue between them would be a personal one rather than a legal one. It was, as always, a test of wills. Was the deputy's determination to bring him to justice as strong as Ken Rex's determination to make him regret it? No.

So as the trial date approached, the witnesses who were scheduled to testify about the barroom brawl began to balk one by one. They balked for good reason. Ken Rex kept the pressure on them, and the climax of his effort was that the tavern got shot up in rip-roaring fashion in the middle of the night, by person or persons unknown.

On the day of the trial Ken Rex's lawyer worked a last-minute plea bargain in which the bribery charge was reduced to a misdemeanor. The original charges were dismissed because of the failure of witnesses to appear. The judge fined Ken Rex five hundred dollars and turned him loose. The disposition of the case set a pattern: He was never to serve a jail term, not even a suspended sentence.

The next felony case against Ken Rex was in Nodaway County in 1973. It followed the pattern of the first so closely that it might have been called a sequel. This was the case in which Ken Rex was charged with raping Trena McCloud and deliberately burning down her family's house.

Again, another charge was added to the original ones; this time it was "exhibiting a dangerous weapon." Skidmore made a sexual joke out of that, but the charge actually involved an attempt by Ken Rex to intimidate the officer who came to arrest him. The tactic worked.

As in the St. Joe case, witnesses began knuckling under to Ken Rex's pressure. Only this time, instead of a bar getting shot up, a house got burned down. Again the main charges against Ken Rex were dropped, and for the same reason. The additional charge was also dropped when the arresting officer failed to testify against Ken Rex.

For the second time within a year Ken Rex walked out of court a free man, only this time he didn't even have to pay a fine, and he had a blushing bride to show for all the trouble.

Ken Rex would be arrested at least five other times for cattle rustling, but there would not be a conviction or even a trial. Meanwhile the livestock thefts in the area climbed outrageously until Nodaway County would have six times more thefts than any other county in the state.

A cryptic entry for 1974 shows that in March Ken Rex was charged in Nodaway County with "molestation." Although the courthouse will not confirm or deny any details of the charge, this apparently was the case of the young girl who had to be committed to the state mental institution. The official result of the case was *nolle prosequi*—"not prosecuted." Records of the case are permanently sealed.

In the summer of 1976, when Americans were celebrating the Bicentennial, Ken Rex put on his own kind of fireworks display—with a shotgun. It was a scary show that brought him to trial for the first time on a charge of assault with intent to kill.

His victim this time was Romaine Henry, a farmer who lived near the McElroy place a few miles south of Skidmore. Henry wasn't some simpering little old farmer in a straw hat. A burly man then in his early forties, Henry gave away very little to Ken Rex in either size or strength. He wasn't a man who could be intimidated easily.

Romaine Henry told the story of his encounter with Ken Rex again and again to the reporters who swarmed into Skidmore after Judgment Day, and each time he told it he seemed more incredulous that it turned out the way it did. It is a chilling story, even a number of years after it happened and with Ken Rex safely moldering in his grave, so it's no wonder that it frightened Skidmore so badly at the time.

JUDGMENT DAY

This is the story that Henry told:

He was working in the shop of his farm one day that summer in 1976 when he heard gunshots from a grove of trees nearby. He hopped into his pickup and went to investigate. He found Ken Rex standing beside the road with a shotgun. Henry stopped the pickup beside Ken Rex—so that Ken Rex was framed by the window opposite the driver's side. Henry had known Ken Rex since childhood and they had never had any run-ins before.

Henry leaned over to ask Ken Rex what the shooting was all about, since this wasn't hunting season. He said Ken Rex started whispering and mumbling—he seemed to be making some accusations. Then all of a sudden he jerked open the pickup door and poked the shotgun into the cab. Henry said that he started denying the accusations, which were strange and puzzling, but that Ken Rex cut him off in an angry, raised voice:

"You're lying. You're the son of a bitch that's been driving by my house."

The next thing Henry heard was a loud blast. The shot blew the pickup door open on Henry's side of the cab and put fifteen pellets in his belly. Henry gasped in astonishment and cowered against the loosened truck door as the concussive ringing rattled his head.

He said Ken Rex then put the gun barrel flush against his right temple and held it there for a minute, just tormenting him. Then Ken Rex pulled the gun barrel back a few inches and aimed a couple inches to one side and pulled the trigger again.

This second discharge flayed Henry's cheek, and blood from this wound began to rain down and commingle with the blood soaking up through his shirt from the stomach wounds. As Ken Rex pulled the shotgun back and started reloading, Henry seized the moment to throw the truck in gear, stomp on the accelerator, wheel the truck around, and speed back to his house in a panic.

It seems obvious that Ken Rex was torturing Henry instead of trying to kill him straight off, but the official charge entered against him was assault with intent to kill. The case would take thirteen months to come to trial— time enough for all Henry's wounds to heal and his resolve to harden. This time surely Ken Rex had gone too far. If Romaine Henry would just hang in there, if he could make it through the long wait and bring Ken Rex to trial, then the court would put an end to Ken Rex's reign of terror.

Henry said that Ken Rex kept the pressure on him during all those months with night-riding, spotlighting windows, and shadowing him as he worked in the grainfields on his farm. This time Ken Rex tried nothing drastic like shooting up Henry's house or burning it down. He realized that such measures wouldn't be necessary.

The Kansas City lawyer got a change of venue for the trial. It was held in a county many miles away from Skidmore. The lawyer plotted an ingenious defense. For one thing, two Iowa carpenters would turn up to testify that Ken Rex was with them at the time the shooting occurred. For another, the lawyer would attack Henry's credibility on grounds that Henry was "a convicted criminal" while Ken Rex, as a matter of fact, was not. (The plea-bargained five-hundred-dollar fine had been cleared from Ken Rex's record by a legal procedure.)

Henry did have a criminal record, all right. As a youngster he had been involved in a fistfight; there was an assault conviction in youth court, and Henry had to pay a ten-dollar fine. Ken Rex's Kansas City lawyer dwelt on that record, knowing that the prosecution couldn't reciprocate by citing Ken Rex's many felony arrests. Since Ken Rex had never been convicted of a crime, the prosecution couldn't even *mention* his criminal record.

The lawyer was so smooth that by the end of the trial, Henry said, you might have thought that Ken Rex had been the injured party. If the trial had gone on much longer, Henry later told Skidmore friends over coffee at Mom's Cafe, he might have wound up believing he had shot himself.

To jurors unacquainted with Ken Rex's background, Henry's bizarre story must have sounded preposterous. In the end those jurors decided against the "convicted criminal" and in favor of the soft-spoken and (for all they knew) law-abiding farmer with the credible alibi corroborated by two apparently earnest witnesses. Ken Rex went free again.

After the trial Ken Rex continued to badger Romaine Henry. Among other things, Henry told of Ken Rex's following him into his grainfields and taking a shot at him with a rifle. He said he heard the bullet whiz over his head. He didn't report the incident. He figured that if the legal system was such as to allow a man to blast him twice at point-blank range with a shotgun, it surely wouldn't do anything about one harmless little potshot.

Skidmore was just as dazed as Henry by the outcome of the trial. The community had followed the case closely, and it drew a couple of conclusions from Ken Rex's easy acquittal.

One was that the legal system wasn't going to deliver Skidmore from the growing threat that Ken Rex represented. For the first time one of Ken Rex's victims had forced a felony case against him through to the bitter end, and the only difference in the outcome had been that in addition to Ken Rex's harassing the victim before and after the trial, Ken Rex's lawyer got to humble the victim *during* the trial.

In effect, it was the victim who was put on trial—at least his good name was—while the cockeyed legal system carefully shielded the accused from any damaging exposure. That was the consensus arrived at by Skidmore, and the town shook its collective head and wondered just whose side the legal system was on.

The other conclusion that Skidmore drew was that Ken Rex had become a truly dangerous man. He had been fearsome enough before, but up to now Skidmore had been able to rationalize his behavior to an extent and to hope that he would mellow in his ways as he grew older. Always before, his ruthless actions had been in keeping with his determination to be a peerless outlaw, a recognized tough, an acknowledged stud. People could understand that, even if they didn't approve of it. But this attack on Romaine Henry was something else. It was an act of wanton violence, seemingly done for the pure enjoyment of it.

There was a rumor in Skidmore that, contrary to what Henry said, there had been friction between him and Ken Rex over a woman. But even if Skidmore tried to believe the story, it still couldn't justify the horrifying response to such a mundane provocation. A man who would do what Ken Rex had done to Romaine Henry was capable of doing anything to anybody, of reacting with unbelievable savagery to the most innocuous word or deed.

JUDGMENT DAY

As it turned out, that's exactly what Ken Rex showed he was capable of in the spring of 1980.

*

It was April, and Ken Rex and Trena had brought some of the younger McElroy children into Skidmore. One of their stops was the B&B Grocery, Ernest and Lois Bowenkamp, proprietors. Ken Rex and Trena bought a few items and took them out to the pickup, while the kids, as kids will do, dawdled in the candy section of the store.

A fuss developed between eight-year-old Tonia McElroy and one of her sisters about which of them their father had told could have a piece of candy. Tonia settled the matter by popping the disputed morsel into her mouth. A clerk in the store happened to be watching and told the child she would have to pay for the candy. There was a small scene which ended with Tonia running out of the store in tears.

Trena and Ken Rex stormed back into the store moments later and started berating the clerk: "What do you mean accusing my kid of stealing? My kids don't steal! They never stole nothing in their lives! By God, you don't know who you're up against here! You better apologize right now or you'll be sorry!"

Lois Bowenkamp heard the commotion from another part of the store and came over to see what was going on. She couldn't get a word in, though, because of the way Ken Rex and Trena were letting the clerk have it.

"I'm just trying to do my job," the clerk kept trying to say.

Now Lois's hackles were raised. A pleasant person of about forty who usually minded her own business, Lois

84

was not one to stand by and watch others being abused. She tried to defend the clerk. Ernest Bowenkamp, who usually works behind the meat counter at the back of the store, now came up front, and he, too, interceded for the clerk.

The argument was soon hot and heavy, and of course one-sided. The Bowenkamps tried to smooth the ruffled McElroy feathers. In a final attempt at appeasement, both Lois and the clerk apologized for hurting the little girl's feelings. But Ken Rex and Trena still left in a huff.

This was the only trouble the Bowenkamps had ever had with Ken Rex and his brood, and even by Skidmore standards the incident was a trivial one. It unsettled the store owners for a time because they knew of Ken Rex's volatile temper, but after a few days they decided that nothing else was going to come of it.

But the incident must have preyed on Ken Rex's mind. He was quick to rise to any challenge, and maybe he thought he hadn't risen to this one. It could be that the incident roiled an old memory of an unavenged slight when he was his daughter's age. Did Ernest Bowenkamp remind him of those men who had laughed at Tony McElroy's "mamma's boy" stories all those years ago? Did something in Bowenkamp's tone suggest to Ken Rex that the grocer looked down on the McElroy clan?

At this stage, too, Ken Rex was beginning to be troubled by self-doubts about his ability to keep his tough-guy reputation. He was forty-six and he looked it, what with all his added weight, sagging jowls, and bags under the eyes.

In any case, it was Bowenkamp, not the clerk, who became the target of Ken Rex's smoldering resentment.

Three months went by before Ken Rex was in the B&B

Grocery again—and at that time he entered through the back door—but meanwhile he did find ways to give Bowenkamp a hard time.

One day later that spring Ken Rex was driving past the store when he spotted Bowenkamp on the street with some other men. He slowed his pickup and called out to the older man:

"Hey, Bo, are you still the boss in there? Or is that woman?"

Bowenkamp, embarrassed in front of the others, replied that he reckoned he was still the boss.

"If your old lady's still the boss," Ken Rex went on, "why don't she come out here and whip Trena's ass? I'll give her a hundred-dollar bill if she can do it."

Bowenkamp avoided trouble that time by retiring back into the store. He dodged some other attempts at provocation as the weeks went on. But on July 8, 1980, Ken Rex didn't let him dodge.

Ken Rex was in Skidmore late that afternoon, drinking beer at D&G's. He apparently had been brooding hard that day about his failure to square matters with Bowenkamp. At least two witnesses would later testify that they heard him mutter threats against Bowenkamp in the tavern.

He left the tavern about sundown and went to his pickup parked outside. It's only a few steps from the tavern across the alley to the loading dock behind the B&B Grocery, and Ken Rex saw Bowenkamp out there on that loading dock.

Just minutes later Skidmore heard the thundering *whoom* of a shotgun.

It came from inside the grocery, which was already closed for the day.

Ernest Bowenkamp was lying on the floor inside the store, alone, shot in the throat and bleeding badly, while Ken Rex returned to his pickup and roared off out of town in the gathering dusk.

Someone who heard the shot alerted Dave Dunbar, the town marshal. He ran to the store and found Bowenkamp convulsing on the floor, trying to tell the name of his attacker but unable to because the shot had damaged his larynx.

The marshal took him to the hospital in Maryville. The wounded man was later transferred to the Methodist Medical Center in St. Joe, where he lay near death in the intensive care unit for two days before he began to recover.

Bowenkamp had taken the wadding of the shell and eleven pellets in the throat. He would be speechless for several months during his painful convalescence. In addition, his left side had been severely damaged, and for months he was unable to lift his left arm.

But he survived because most of the discharge just missed him, obliterating several ceiling panels behind him. In that respect, the shooting was similar to that of Romaine Henry; it was again as if Ken Rex had shot not to kill but to maim and torture, to mete out some of his own brand of distorted justice.

A warrant was issued in Maryville for Ken Rex's arrest, and he was apprehended that evening by the Missouri Highway Patrol about thirty-four miles from Skidmore in another county. By the time he was returned to Maryville, his lawyer was at the courthouse waiting to bail him out. He posted bond of thirty thousand dollars and went home.

JUDGMENT DAY

Two nights later Ken Rex was back in Skidmore. When he walked into D&G's, the people in the place were shocked into silence by his presence. Here was the man who had shot and almost killed Ernest Bowenkamp, but he was free as a bird while old "Bo" was lying in intensive care down in St. Joe.

It only took the tavern a few minutes to clear out, but before people could get out of his way, Ken Rex made some bold statements. He seemed angry that he had been arrested. He warned the whole town that he would deal with anyone who took Bowenkamp's side just as sternly as he had dealt with Bowenkamp himself. Hurrying out of the bar, people saw one of Ken Rex's women in a "backup" truck, holding a shotgun at the ready.

Sentiment in Skidmore really began to harden against Ken Rex now. A "wanted" poster started appearing on barn walls and trees and utility poles in and around town. It sported a crude caricature of Ken Rex and a list of some of his suspected offenses—rape, arson, larceny, attempted murder. It was the handiwork of irate citizens who nonetheless hid behind the safety of anonymity.

Skidmore showed its revulsion in other passive ways too. Men started avoiding the tavern when Ken Rex was drinking there, which was often. They cleared out of the place when he came in. D&G's trade suffered and the co-owner of the tavern, Del Clement, finally asked Ken Rex not to come around the place. Ken Rex just laughed and kept on drinking.

The tavern was his campaign headquarters, and, in retrospect, the question was just what kind of campaign he was waging. It never occurred to Skidmore that it was anything other than one of intimidation and harassment, a campaign to sow fear. And Skidmore has tales aplenty to buttress that view:

QUICKSAND YEARS

—One night Ken Rex came into the tavern, set a paper sack on the bar, shook out several bills—fifties and hundreds—and put a hunting knife on the pile. He turned to a man at the counter and told him the money was his if he would take the knife over to the grocery store, pretend to trip, and "run old man Bowenkamp through."

—Another night at the bar, Ken Rex sent Trena out to the pickup to fetch another paper bag. This one contained a .38-caliber pistol; he took the .38 out, twirled it around like a gunslinger, and pointed it at the bartender. "One of us ain't going to be around much longer," he said. It was dialogue right out of *Shane.*

—Pastor Tim Warren of the Skidmore Christian church, who had ignored those husky-voiced telephone threats to stay away from the Bowenkamps, returned from visiting Bowenkamp at the hospital one afternoon to find Ken Rex waiting on the street near the church. Ken Rex was standing beside his pickup with a Thompson submachine gun in one hand and an ammunition clip in the other. Warren managed to slip inside the church without being seen. He composed himself and went back out, circling around so that he had the drop on Ken Rex. He was ready to defend himself and his home if he thought it was coming to that. The two men faced one another and there was a kind of a standoff. Ken Rex just got back in his truck and drove away.

—It was now, in August, that Ken Rex caught Dave Dunbar in the shadows just beyond the Punkin Festival hoopla, poked the shotgun in his belly, and held him in life-and-death suspense for twenty minutes. Dunbar, who was making only $240 a month at his job and had a wife and baby to support, was so unnerved by the incident that he turned in his resignation to Mayor Steve Peter a few weeks later and took a job hooking up cable TV in and around Maryville. Steve called a town council meeting to hire a new marshal, but the council couldn't find anyone else who would take the job. So Skidmore lost its last resident representative of the law and felt more vulnerable than ever.

—Lois Bowenkamp later told reporters of the harassment she and her convalescent husband had to endure throughout that long year between the shooting and the trial. It was much the same type that Romaine Henry had experienced—the roaring pickup convoys in the small hours of the night, the spotlights thrown on bedroom windows, the sudden eruption of gunfire, the bellowed threats. Lois wrote urgent letters to county, state, and congressional officials pleading for relief. "Are we to live in fear the rest of our lives?" she asked. She got back sympathetic replies expressing regret and pointing out that the matter was a local one that the courts would have to handle.

During those months between the shooting and the trial, Ken Rex was waging a campaign of fear, all right—goading, taunting, scaring Skidmore. But what was he trying to prove by it? What was he hoping to accomplish?

Was his object to frighten the Bowenkamps and all their supporters and would-be supporters so badly that they would finally drop the charge against him? He had used that technique to beat so many raps before, and Skidmore had no reason to suppose he was up to anything different.

But there is something curiously unconvincing and insufficient about that interpretation. Some of the incidents in this case just don't fit that interpretation.

QUICKSAND YEARS

The incidents with the .38 pistol in the tavern and with the submachine gun on the street are almost like omens, foreshadowings of an episode that would occur months later in the countdown to Judgment Day. This was a truly strange episode that would suggest that Ken Rex was pushing for a showdown, all right, but not with Skidmore. In this larger view, he was pushing for a showdown with fate, and trying to goad Skidmore into becoming fate's reluctant instrument.

Although Ken Rex shot Ernest Bowenkamp on July 8, 1980, his trial couldn't be docketed until the fall term of the circuit court in Maryville. That gave him three months to work in his own special way at cross-examining the prospective witnesses against him. And, as in the Romaine Henry case, his lawyers would use various court-room maneuvers to buy him additional time.

Richard Gene McFadin, the Kansas City lawyer who had served him so effectively and faithfully before, first filed a petition for a change of venue, contending that Ken Rex couldn't get a fair trial in Maryville. The motion was routinely granted and the trial was delayed until January 1981. The site was changed to the courthouse at Bethany, a small town in Harrison County about seventy miles east of Skidmore.

McFadin then brought in another defense attorney, Richard Webster, a state senator, as an associate in the case. That, too, was a traditional ploy to buy more time from the court. Since Webster was a member of the state General Assembly, which would be in session throughout the spring of 1981, the trial had to be delayed again. It was reset for June 25, 1981, more than fifty weeks from the time of the shooting. All these maneuvers did suggest that Ken Rex and his lawyers were concerned that the Bowenkamps and their Skidmore supporters wouldn't be pushovers. Old Bo was refusing to crack under the strain.

While Ken Rex kept the pressure on, something happened down at St. Joe early that summer which heightened the tension in Skidmore: A cleanup man at the Hickory Bar was found beaten to death. The Hickory, a bar on night-spot row in St. Joe, was one of Ken Rex's regular haunts.

There was nothing to tie Ken Rex to the crime, but word around Skidmore was that he had killed the man. That belief added to the anxiety of the Bowenkamps and their Skidmore well-wishers as they counted off the days and nights leading up to June 25.

*

Bethany is an hour and a half east of the Nodaway Empire, an up-and-down drive across the rich, rolling landscape, directly into the morning sun. You could drive all day and into the night before you came to a city of any size, and that would be Chicago. Bethany is a slow-paced farming town of about three thousand people, its small business district huddled around a town square centered by the Harrison County Courthouse, which could be a twin of the courthouse at Maryville.

Ken Rex seldom ranged into Harrison County, so there was no pretrial stir in Bethany, and a business-as-usual atmosphere prevailed on the morning of June 25, 1981.

Bailiff Merrill R. Klever, a veteran Harrison County deputy sheriff, showed up first at the courtroom that morning and waited at the defense table for Ken Rex to arrive and surrender himself to the court. Sheriff Leon Riggs came in next with the circuit clerk and the court recorder. They stood chatting while some early-bird members of the jury panel filed in, followed soon by a small contingent from Skidmore: Ernest and Lois Bowenkamp; Ronald Charles and Eldon Everhart, two witnesses for the prosecution; Pastor Tim Warren, whose steadfast support of the Bowenkamps during their year-long ordeal had even included standing guard at their store on occasion; and a few other friends of the store owners.

At this point lawyer McFadin entered briskly, a picture of confidence and cosmopolitan charm, and stopped to chat amiably with the circuit clerk. And then came the other defense lawyers—Richard Webster and a McFadin associate from Kansas City named Charles Spooner.

Only after Prosecutor David Baird and Nodaway County Sheriff Danny Estes had taken their places did Ken Rex and Trena make their entrance. They came down the middle aisle of the courtroom and made quite an impression. Ken Rex was dressed in a new suit, with white shirt, studs, and a dark tie. Trena was wearing a new outfit and a perky smile. When Ken Rex took his place at the defense table, Trena slipped in directly behind him in the first row of the gallery.

The Skidmore contingent clustered on the other side of the courtroom.

No one on the jury panel had heard of Ken Rex, his reputation or his legend, so there was no difficulty in seating a jury, and the morning passed tediously as the lawyers presented their opening arguments.

Prosecutor Baird called his first witness—Sheriff Estes—early that afternoon. Baird put a few questions to Estes, and then asked him to recount his investigation of the shooting of Ernest Bowenkamp. Estes identified the shotgun used in the shooting as belonging to Ken Rex McElroy. It had been confiscated by the Missouri Highway Patrol, he said, at the time of Ken Rex's arrest.

Then Ronald Charles and Eldon Everhart testified that they had seen Ken Rex in Skidmore shortly before the shooting, and both said they had heard him utter threats against Bowenkamp. Their testimony was strenuously challenged by the defense lawyers, who characterized it as personal prejudice and hearsay.

Baird then called Bowenkamp himself to the stand. The old grocer seemed a bit bewildered by the formalities of the proceeding, but he didn't waver—even under heavy, antagonistic cross-examination—in his account of the shooting and the events leading up to it. He related the "candy episode" and told of the subsequent encounters with Ken Rex, when the latter seemed to be trying to bait him. Baird then asked him to describe the events of the evening of July 8, 1980. Speaking in a voice still gravelly from his wounds, Bowenkamp gave this account:

After closing the B&B late in the afternoon, he went out behind the store to work on the broken air-conditioning unit. It was about 7:45 P.M., but there was still daylight, when Ken Rex pulled his pickup into the alley beside the B&B loading dock and stopped. Ken Rex got out of the truck and stood there rolling up his sleeves. Bowenkamp told him the truck was blocking a private drive and asked him to move the truck. Ken Rex said: "Do you want to fight?"

Bowenkamp declined the invitation and went into the store, as he had done on other occasions when Ken Rex tried to hassle him. He said he picked up a butcher knife and started cutting up some cardboard boxes, busying himself in this way while waiting for Ken Rex to be gone. But this time Ken Rex didn't leave. Bowenkamp heard a noise and looked around. Ken Rex had opened the back door and was standing there pointing a shotgun at him. Bowenkamp started to order Ken Rex to leave, but Ken Rex leveled the shotgun at him and pulled the trigger.

Bowenkamp matter-of-factly described his wounds and the treatment he received for them.

On cross-examination McFadin concentrated his questioning on the butcher knife. Wasn't it true that the old grocer had grabbed up the knife and "gone after" Ken Rex with it, advancing on him with the knife held above his head in threatening fashion? No, Bowenkamp replied. And no matter how much McFadin persisted, Bowenkamp continued to deny that he had threatened Ken Rex with the knife or had advanced on him with it.

It was late afternoon when McFadin called Ken Rex to testify in his own behalf.

Ken Rex sat quietly in the witness chair, gazing serenely at his hands folded in his lap, as McFadin asked the routine preliminary questions. He leaned forward slightly, showing no anxiety, when McFadin got to the pertinent questions. He didn't dispute ownership of the shotgun; he admitted that he was present when Bowenkamp was shot. He didn't deny that he had pulled the trigger. But his version of the shooting and the events leading up to it was this:

He said he pulled into the alley beside the loading dock because a stalled vehicle had blocked traffic on the main street of Skidmore and he couldn't get around. He saw Bowenkamp on the loading dock and Bowenkamp called out something to him that he didn't hear, so he killed the motor and leaned out to ask Bowenkamp what it was he had said. Bowenkamp told him to move the truck, and he made an effort to but the truck wouldn't start. So he got out of the truck, saw some youngsters nearby, went over to chat with them briefly, gave them some pocket change so they could buy themselves soft drinks, and returned to his truck.

As he started to climb back into the truck, he saw Bowenkamp coming at him with the butcher knife raised threateningly. He fell into the truck, fearing for his life, grabbed the shotgun off the gun rack, and fired quickly and desperately, not even taking time to aim. Bowenkamp retreated into the store and Ken Rex got the truck started and drove away.

When Baird cross-examined him, Ken Rex denied that he had left the scene of the shooting to avoid arrest and prosecution. He said he had no idea that the shot had struck Bowenkamp, and he learned that Bowenkamp had been wounded only when the arresting officers told him. He said he then submitted to arrest without resistance.

Testimony having been concluded on the first day of the trial, attorneys for both sides made their closing statements the next morning, June 26. Judge J. Morgan Donelson began giving instructions to the jury shortly before noon. After a lunch break, the jury began its deliberations at 1:20 P.M. Not two hours had passed before it returned with a verdict:

Guilty of second-degree assault.

Recommended sentence: two years in prison.

Deputy Klever, the bailiff, said Ken Rex and his lawyers had appeared confident throughout the trial that they would win the case.

"I think they thought they could come in here and make a big show and overpower everybody," Klever said. "All during the trial, Ken Rex sat there staring at the witnesses or staring at the jury. When he got up to testify, he hardly spoke above a whisper, though he didn't seem a bit scared. The judge had to ask him to speak up a couple of times."

Klever said Ken Rex got fidgety near the end of the trial. "He kept leaning back and whispering to Trena. Just when the jury was coming in, I heard him tell her, 'If this thing don't turn out right, you know what to do.' "

As the jury foreman was announcing the verdict, Ken Rex turned and looked at Trena. Klever said she jumped up and made a big show of running out of the courtroom. Not walking, but running, and attracting everyone's attention.

"I don't know what she was up to," he said. "Maybe those jury members found out that night."

The Skidmore contingent showed no jubilation when the verdict was announced. Second-degree assault was the lowest-level felony misdemeanor, and the recommendation for a two-year prison term was an insult to Ernest Bowenkamp, who had suffered so much physically and emotionally. With early parole, Ken Rex would probably spend less time in prison than Bowenkamp had spent in the hospital. The Skidmore people avoided looking in Ken Rex's direction when they arose and silently walked out of the courtroom.

But what they did not know was that the case was not yet concluded. The defense lawyers went up to the judge and informed him of their intention to appeal the conviction; pending the appeal, they asked Judge Donelson to free Ken Rex on bond. The judge gave them forty-five days to file the appeal and he set a bond of forty thousand dollars, which Ken Rex posted immediately.

For another month and a half at least he would be as free as ever.

The jurors didn't know about Ken Rex, his reputation and his legend, but Harrison County Sheriff Leon Riggs did. A young lawman who gives the impression of being a stable and tireless worker, Riggs talked about Ken Rex.

"Hell, you couldn't be a law officer in this part of the country and not know about Ken Rex," he said. When he and his deputies attended regional meetings with lawmen from neighboring counties and states, one inevitable topic of conversation was Ken Rex. "They knew about him all over. Ken Rex liked to be known. He lived on it."

Because of what he knew, Riggs took some special precautions during the trial. After the first day's testimony, he escorted the jurors to the town's only motel and locked them in. He and his deputies stood guard all night at the motel and allowed no telephone calls into the jury members' rooms. The first night passed without incident.

But the next night, after the jurors had returned to their homes, they began to get anonymous telephone calls asking them why they had found an innocent man guilty. It wasn't just one call, but a succession of them throughout the night, in which the words spoken by the husky voice grew more somber and ominous with each call.

Several of the jurors reported the calls to Sheriff Riggs. They told him they couldn't identify the caller or callers, but some were certain that the voice wasn't Ken Rex's. The sheriff said the calls had one macabre feature in common—the threat of "rattlesnake punishment."

The jurors were told that sometime soon rattlesnake venom would be slipped into their drinking water. And they were also told that they shouldn't be surprised if they woke up in the middle of the night and found a live rattlesnake in bed with them.

"Those people got scared to death overnight," Sheriff Riggs and Deputy Klever said. "They regretted ever having been on that jury. They said they would never have agreed to serve if they had known who this man McElroy really was.

"We told them we would try to protect them. But we've got a big county here, almost as big as Nodaway, and we've got our share of rowdies too. We're a three-man staff, that's all, with a lot of little towns just like Skidmore to look after."

The harassment dwindled at Bethany after the first night or two, though. Now the action shifted back to the Nodaway Empire, back to Skidmore, which was almost ready to become a character instead of just a place.

Countdown

"Fear of danger is ten thousand times
more terrifying than danger itself."
—from *Robinson Crusoe* by Daniel Defoe

Prosecutor Baird, who was watching Ken Rex as the verdict was read, said he "remained expressionless."

Bailiff Klever, who had watched him throughout the trial, said that in the moment before he turned to look at Trena, he appeared to be stunned.

One wonders what caused him to start fidgeting just before the jury returned to the courtroom, and what he really thought when that novel word "guilty" vibrated in his eardrums. To know that would be to begin to fathom the mystery of the man.

But there's no way to know; there can only be supposition. And the most likely guess is that there in the courtroom Ken Rex's keen intuition began for the first time to hear distinctly a sound that had been echoing vaguely in the great, labyrinthine emptiness of his soul for a long time now. He knew finally that the sound was the intolerable pealing of a bell.

For some years now Ken Rex had been losing his old magic.

His was a young man's game, and he was forty-seven years old and showing it. His grim, stalking weight of 220 pounds had paunched and pudged up past 260. He looked bloated, his eyes were puffy and swollen, his jowls sagging badly. His flesh gathered up around the rolls of double chins; his shirt gaped apart at the buttons.

The change in appearance was devastating to a man whose power over people depended so much on his forbidding physical presence. Staring people down isn't as easy for an old basset as it is for a young wolf.

And he was not a well man. His drinking, his excess weight, his high blood pressure, his nosebleeds, his blackouts, his frequent gastric disorders, and a variety of other ailments took more and more of a toll as he got older. All through the trial he had coughed; and he took sips constantly from a bottle of cough medicine.

Over the last few years he had been in and out of hospitals, but he wouldn't take care of himself, apparently bent on punishing his body for betraying him in much the same way that he punished his enemies. The terrorizing of his later years—as in his attacks on Romaine Henry and Ernest Bowenkamp—was a sign of a creeping lack of confidence in his ability to intimidate people in the old menacing ways.

Another indication of decline was his increasing reliance on McFadin. Earlier in his career Ken Rex had used his lawyer as another kind of "backup" unit. He was there as a precaution, but overall Ken Rex dealt with his legal problems in his own roughshod way, doing what he had to do to get charges dropped and cases dismissed. In the last two big cases, though, he had to yield control, submit to full trials, and place his fate completely in his lawyer's hands. How he must have hated that. Even Skidmore grudgingly conceded that McFadin was an excellent trial lawyer, but it went against every impulse in Ken Rex's body and soul to depend on anyone for anything, much less for everything.

Now this conviction. It was a nail in the coffin of the image he had tried to project. He had spent his life making a reputation for himself—as a man who had money, and damn anyone who questioned how he got it; as a man who got the women he wanted, and damn anyone who disapproved or got in his way; as a man of power whom none of these hemmers-and-hawers and pussy-whipped shufflers would ever dare laugh at or cross or snub.

He had built that reputation with real deeds, and not with just a lot of bluster and make-believe like his old man. Making and maintaining that reputation—requiring others to concede that he really *was* somebody—surely was the great motivation of his life. But this conviction sounded the knell of that reputation—sounded it clearly, unmistakably, intolerably. If he couldn't negate it or erase it or overcome it somehow, the old geezers idling on the benches in front of the Legion Hall or standing around in the shade of the stock barns or sipping beer and peppermint schnapps at D&G's would laugh when somebody mentioned Ken Rex McElroy, the terror of the territory, done in by a gangly old man, shackled and trundled off to the state pen. He would be remembered as a caricature of his father. Not a somebody, a nobody.

He couldn't live with that. But there it was. What was he supposed to do about it?

In the moment after the verdict was read, Ken Rex must have realized what he had known for some time now without knowing he knew it. He realized what Jesse James must have realized after the bloody ambush at Northfield, Minnesota, and what Black Hawk realized when he got his first full view of the iron might of the United States Army:

That time for him had just about run out.

So Ken Rex ignored his lawyer's advice to lie low and stay out of Skidmore during the appeal period. In no time he was right back at the bar in D&G's. He did some talking there about how Skidmore was going to pay, but most likely that was just a way of running some of the old Ken Rex bluff up the flagpole. He was feeling out the situation and waiting.

Skidmore, for its part, was assessing him too. Its reading of the situation was this: With a minimum of forty-five more days and long nights in which to work his vengeance, Ken Rex would have plenty of time to make the town sweat—to force people to lie awake nights wondering what, wondering when.

In this tense measuring of one another, Ken Rex and Skidmore were like the combatants in a popular form of trial-by-ordeal that existed in these parts in the early frontier days. In such an event, two antagonists would be stripped naked, each given a bowie knife, and thrown into an empty, pitch-black room. Whoever came out alive—if either of them did—was allowed to go free. Ken Rex was the old champ at this kind of psychological warfare, but in the wake of the verdict at Bethany, Skidmore would no longer be his fall guy and patsy. Skidmore was molding itself into shape as a challenger to be reckoned with, whether it knew it yet or not. Old champ and new challenger were completely in the dark about one another's intentions, each waiting to see what the other's next move would be, each hoping for a show of weakness, a careless mistake.

Then it was the fourth night after the conviction—the evening of Tuesday, June 30. Events of this night would lead four citizens of Skidmore—Pete Ward, his sons Wesley and Wilson, and Gary Dowling—to sign an official complaint with Prosecutor Baird against Ken Rex, for violation of the terms of his appeal bond.

According to the statements signed by Dowling and the Wards, Ken Rex lumbered into D&G's again, and this time Trena was behind him—an oddity for her because she usually waited outside in the pickup for him as his backup. But now she followed Ken Rex to his customary place at the end of the long bar, where he always stood with his back to the wall. There were about a dozen men in the tavern that night. They watched Trena this time instead of Ken Rex, for she was toting an M-1 rifle that had a gleaming bayonet affixed to it.

Settled at the bar, Ken Rex started laughing. He looked all around the place, as if to get everyone's attention, and then he signaled Trena.

"Hold that thing up," he said to her.

He took a swig of beer and seemed to study the rifle she was displaying. All eyes in the bar were on it. For another moment Ken Rex appeared to be thinking. He took another swig of beer, laughed, and reached quickly to snatch the rifle from Trena. Addressing all in the tavern, Ken Rex said:

"You see this? I'm going to fill old man Bowenkamp full

of holes with it. And then I'm going to turn the bastard over and stick this bayonet up his ass."

There was no laughter in the bar except for Ken Rex's. The others didn't respond as they might have during the past ten or twenty years by humoring the bully until they could get out of his sight. Now they gave no indication that they thought his remarks were either scary or funny. But they did give him their attention—they stared at him in icy silence.

Finally a man at the other end of the bar stood up and defiantly pointed a finger at Ken Rex. He spoke in a controlled, unwavering voice: "You're full of crap, mister, if you think you're going to do that."

This was Pete Ward, a Skidmore resident, a member of the town council. As he and Ken Rex faced each other, the marked contrast between them was apparent. Pete Ward was slender, taller than Ken Rex, with well-groomed white hair and a pencil-thin mustache. He gave the appearance of being an educated, articulate gentleman. There was no fear of Ken Rex in his face, only contempt and a composed resistance.

"You're full of bullshit if you think you'll ever do that," Ward added for emphasis.

If Ken Rex was surprised, he didn't let it show. He studied Ward with that narrowed, withering gaze of his. Then he said something odd.

"Just whose side are you on?" he asked.

"Not yours, that's for damn sure," Ward shot back.

For a time it appeared to the others in the bar that the two men might have a go at one another right there. But it wasn't time yet. Myth-sized events proceed according to their own incalculable timing, and the struggle between Ken Rex and Skidmore wouldn't be hurried to a premature climax. It was Ken Rex who backed off and let the crisis pass.

Ward, satisfied that he had won the point, left the tavern with his two sons, Wesley and Wilson. A friend of theirs named Gary Dowling left with them. They departed from the bar with a purpose—to contact Prosecutor Baird at Maryville and report that Ken Rex had handled a rifle in the tavern, thus violating the terms of his appeal bond.

Ken Rex's taking that rifle from Trena was as momentous a turning point in his career as the reading of the verdict had been just four days before. With that action, he set in motion a series of events that led directly and swiftly to his downfall. It was a flagrant violation of his bond, and all Skidmore had to do was report it and verify it with witnesses, plenty of whom were on hand, and Ken Rex would go directly to jail.

He must have known that. Else why would he have had Trena bring the rifle into the tavern? Why wouldn't he have just brought it in himself? The way he handled the whole thing was almost theatrical, as if he wanted to be certain that everyone in the place understood that he knew the law and was determined to flout it.

It was a peculiar incident, but Skidmore didn't puzzle over it. In Skidmore's view, it was Ken Rex strutting his old stuff, intent on showing everyone that just because the law had stung him once, he didn't intend to change his ways. It was Ken Rex testing the local waters to see how much the conviction had damaged his king-of-the-hill reputation. Skidmore saw his action as another provocation, which, if he got away with it, would no doubt embolden him to meaner measures.

But was Skidmore reading him right? If that bell was

tolling inside his head, maybe he was looking for a way to force the issue with Skidmore. Maybe he was trying to hasten to a conclusion a struggle in which he had already sensed that he was doomed.

A clue might have been his odd response when Ward pointed that finger and called his hand. *"Just whose side are you on?"* he had said. What an amazing utterance! Ken Rex, the old terror, answering a public dare with a question! And not even a menacing question, but an irrelevant one. A question that diffused tension rather than heightening it, throwing an air of absurdity over the whole episode, as if Ken Rex was merely acting out a mandatory scene that no longer interested him because he had realized, once the incident started, that the time wasn't yet right for the climactic showdown.

If there was any sense at all to the question, it was of a subtle nature that Skidmore wasn't ready to grasp yet. "Just whose side are you on?" meant that Ken Rex saw the issue in terms of Him versus Them. But Skidmore hadn't coalesced yet into a single-minded character of this drama, a character equal to a fair-fight showdown with a legendary criminal, a character with the guts and the willpower and maybe even the madness to face Ken Rex down and do what had to be done to stop the tolling of that intolerable bell. If this interpretation is correct, then "Just whose side are you on?" was an expression of impatience—his way of saying, "Why don't you guys get your side together so we can get on with this thing and get it over with?"

In a way, those four men did what Ken Rex wanted. They contacted Prosecutor Baird that same evening after leaving the tavern, and Baird filed a petition with the court at Bethany, asking for a hearing to revoke Ken

Rex's bond. Baird supported the petition with the signatures of the four—the three Wards and Dowling.

The court set the hearing for July 10 in Bethany. It would be ten days away.

A surge of something resembling optimism or hope went through Skidmore. Ten more days—not an interminable forty-five—and the town wouldn't have Ken Rex to kick it around anymore.

Relief was finally in sight. The light at the end of the long dark tunnel. Ten more days.

That same evening, Baird contacted the Missouri Highway Patrol and asked that a trooper be sent to keep watch in Skidmore. The trooper kept watch, as instructed, and Skidmore was as ghostly quiet as the surrounding cornfields, over which the hunter bullbats swooped with silent wing.

But the next night the trooper was gone. And to many people in Skidmore, even ten more days of Ken Rex seemed an eternity, and that light at the end of the tunnel seemed as far away somehow as the buffalo.

*

During the harrowing days and nights leading up to July 10 Skidmore was under a great strain not so much because it was struggling with Ken Rex McElroy but with his legend.

Skidmore had created that legend, but Ken Rex had cultivated it; he had convinced people that there was no crime and no atrocity that he wasn't capable of. Now, with time running out on him—the last days and hours and minutes ticking away before he would go to prison—Skidmore imagined that he would be out to wreak a culminating vengeance.

During the few times he appeared at D&G's, he sounded one refrain over and over: "Anybody who thinks I'm going to prison is crazy as hell. That'll never happen. Never!" That was a simple prophecy, an intuitive statement of fact, but to Skidmore it was a dire promise. Here was a man who the town believed had raped, tortured, mutilated, maimed, and plundered. And all of those past deeds seemed just a prologue to what he might do during the countdown to Judgment Day.

The strain was greater than ever now because Skidmore could no longer conscientiously avoid taking a stand as a community against him. He had picked on people in and around Skidmore for decades, and never once had the town rallied behind one of his victims. Not even when it came to the Bowenkamps had it openly objected; the couple received expressions of support and encouragement all right, but with few exceptions that support had been privately pledged and discreetly expressed.

Throughout the years Skidmore had peeked through the blinds, made excuses, blamed the system, shaken its head, and wished that somebody would *do* something. Now somebody had. And it wasn't just one of Ken Rex's victims pleading vainly for justice. It was four men who had taken the initiative against Ken Rex on behalf of the whole town.

Four was a formidable number of challengers to have standing up to Ken Rex. And this case wouldn't be dragging on for months and years, giving Ken Rex time to work over his antagonists one by one in his inimitable way. The matter would be over and done with within a few days. Skidmore couldn't dodge this one. It could either get behind these four men, throw off the yoke of fear and frustration, and rid itself of Ken Rex's domination once and for all—or it could close the blinds again.

Even townspeople who had never been subjected to direct threats from Ken Rex now felt the pressure to join the revolt. The strain was particularly hard on them during this period. They had managed to stay out of Ken Rex's way all these years by following a live-and-let-live policy. If they chimed in now, weren't they exposing themselves to dreadful retaliations—to rapes and shot-gunnings, to snakes in the mailbox and breasts delivered C.O.D.?

But Skidmore had incentives that it had never had before. Ken Rex was on the defensive, the case against him looked like a cinch, and there was safety in numbers. Also, the town had evolved some strong young leadership capable of imbuing it with the requisite spunk.

In April 1980 Skidmore had elected Steve Peter to be its mayor. Steve was a young man with a college education and a reputation for being able to get things done. A withering little town like Skidmore needs someone like Steve Peter as its mayor—someone with the education and exposure, and thus the know-how, and, the townspeople hope, the patience, to be able to deal with the county bureaucrats in Maryville, the state bureaucrats in Jefferson City, and the knotheads in Washington. Someone with a youthful but at the same time realistic enthusiasm for such Skidmore betterment projects as the acquisition of a new fire truck and the building of a new roadside park just outside town on the road to Maryville. Someone with a native's knowledge of the town and yet not entangled in the competitive social, commercial, and political alliances that are the source of endless petty intrigues in every small town. And someone who won't wilt in a crisis like this.

Steve Peter fit the description. And besides, as he said himself, no one else wanted the job.

Steve was a strapping, rawboned civil engineer who manhandled a bulldozer by day and liked to have a beer and shoot some pool in D&G's after work. In his jeans and T-shirt and heavy work shoes, he looked as tough as the unusual tree stumps he collected as a hobby and displayed around the mobile home where he lived with his pretty wife, Kim, and their two little daughters. That a youngster so rough-edged, untalkative, unpretentious, and unambitious could be the town's most prominent public official just goes to show how far Skidmore is from Maryville and the rest of the world.

As mayor, Steve had been involved in a dozen conversations about the need for Skidmore to "do something" about Ken Rex. Had he been more of a politician, he might have exploited the concern. With some timely law-and-order rhetoric, he could have rallied the town into holding a showdown with Ken Rex long before now. But Steve wasn't one to go looking for trouble, and Ken Rex knew that the mayor was somebody he'd better not put to the test.

"My position made it likely that I'd have a run-in with him sooner or later," Steve said after the showdown finally did take place. "And I'd thought a lot about what I would do if that happened. I couldn't see living scared, with the thought of shots coming through the wall at any time. With worrying day and night about what might happen to my wife and the kids. If he bothered my family, I would've gone out and had it out with him."

He left no doubt about what he meant by "having it out" with Ken Rex.

As mayor he felt a similar responsibility to protect and defend the community, but not with the same visceral passion. He was new in his position at the time of the Bowenkamp shooting, and although he thought about trying to rouse some moral support for the old grocer during his year-long ordeal, his full-time job and the incessant routine demands of the mayoralty kept him hopping so that he never got around to dealing with "the Ken Rex problem."

But by the summer of 1981 Steve was more experienced at civic leadership, and the Bowenkamp ordeal had convinced him that Ken Rex's chronic terrorism was a grave threat to his town and its peace of mind. When those four men lodged their complaint against Ken Rex, the mayor took the lead in rallying community support for their cause.

"Those four guys had the guts to stick their necks out," he said. "The least the rest of us could do was stand by them."

Another young man the community would look to during these dark days of the countdown was Pastor Tim Warren. Tim was a big, blocky youngster, too—the same age as the mayor and looking even more of a big bruiser. He had come to Skidmore from Colorado in 1979, and the Skidmore Christian Church was his first pastorate.

No one looking at Pastor Tim would expect him to be a meek theological quibbler, someone who stresses the wimpy side of Jesus Christ. And he didn't seem to be the type of clergyman who would give too much pulpit attention to such principles as loving your enemies, turning the other cheek, and doing good to those who persecute you. Instead, he looked like a two-fisted fire-and-brimstone Bible thumper, more of an Old Testament man, who would scatter the moneylenders in the temple by scaring the living shit out of them.

In fact, Tim was pretty much what he appeared to be. When he talked to reporters after Judgment Day, he professed faith in an unorthodox Trinity. In the face of Ken Rex's intimidation, Pastor Tim said he had come to believe in God, Guns, and Guts. He had shown it too. Ever since those first anonymous threats against him in the summer of 1980, he had kept on guard and had left the members of his growing flock in no doubt that he would stand up to Ken Rex if he crowded him or his parishioners too closely.

His was one of only two churches in Skidmore, and the only active one, really, since the Methodist church didn't even have a resident pastor. His little Christian church wasn't affiliated with the parent national Disciples of Christ denomination—an amiable ecumenical sect—so it could go in whatever direction he led it. Tim's fiery fundamentalism had revitalized the church, and his personal example had stirred a spirit of resistance in his congregation. The people trusted him and would follow where he directed.

Warren was one of the few townspeople who had stood openly on the side of the Bowenkamps, who were members of his church. He had gone so far as to stand guard at their grocery store on the occasion of their ordeal. And then there was the scary incident of Ken Rex's calling at the parsonage with the tommy gun, but backing off when the preacher got the drop on him. As he had done with the young mayor, Ken Rex had tested the preacher and, finding him too worthy a foe, had turned away.

There were others, too—civic leaders who kept a lower profile than the mayor or pastor, but who were ready

114

finally to lend their influence to the cause of delivering Skidmore from the scourge.

So, four solid citizens had taken the lead against Ken Rex, and God and city hall were calling up the reserves. It must have been the most irresistible coalition to hit Skidmore since Populism. Even the most frightened and most lethargic would have been ashamed not to enlist.

In those days between the Bowenkamp trial and July 10, there were several meetings—a few men here, a few men there, over coffee at Mom's, over beer at D&G's, after prayer meeting at the Christian church. Out of these sessions a plan of action emerged.

"We had two goals," Mayor Peter said. "We wanted to show that the whole community supported those four witnesses, and we wanted to make sure that nobody did anything that Ken Rex and his lawyer could use against us to get him off the hook again."

What they decided to do finally was this: Early in the morning on July 10 they would gather at the American Legion Hall, form a caravan, drive ceremoniously over to Bethany, enter the courthouse as a group, and sit together during the bond-revocation hearing. They intended the action as a solid demonstration of community unity and commitment—a demonstration for Ken Rex's benefit as much as for that of the four witnesses against him. They would show Ken Rex, show the court, and show the world where they stood.

And mainly they would show themselves.

It was a naïve plan, which McFadin would be able to undermine simply by requesting a routine postponement of the hearing. It wasn't flashy enough to attract any publicity—who would pay any attention to a bunch of people sitting through a dry court hearing and then going back home?—so its impact would be purely psychological and extremely subtle. And it would be logistically awkward, getting that many people together on a workday.

But if it worked—and maybe even if it didn't—it would answer Ken Rex's question: Just whose side are you on? It would answer it both ways. It would affirm Pete Ward's answer, "Not yours, that's for damn sure!" And it would signal Ken Rex that there finally *was* another side; that he had an opponent now worthy of taking him on, and ready and willing to take his best shots—a single-minded opponent named Skidmore.

Where was Ken Rex while Skidmore was gathering its nerve and its numbers? What was he doing?

As Skidmore was to recall later, he was on the prowl, up to his usual tricks: the roaring McElroy convoys, the spotlights thrown into sleepless bedrooms, the shouted threats, the telephone whispering of impending butcheries. But nothing innovative. Nothing new and God-awful marked his last raging days of freedom.

And that makes one wonder. Could it be that Skidmore remembered more McElroy activity during this time than really happened? Did Skidmore, when it looked back on those few anxious nights, compress into them all the McElroy marauding that had occurred over a number of years? Was it Ken Rex's legend that did most of that last-minute night-riding, which Skidmore needed to pump itself up for the coming showdown? Was some of the final terrorism spun into the legend by the reporters and commentators who came along afterward and needed it to make the course of events more dramatic?

The memories of those days have all been blurred, and it is the myth that triumphs and has its own way. According to the myth, Ken Rex *was* on the prowl, giving it his last best shot. He had precipitated the crisis by handling the rifle in the tavern, and maybe in an obscure, intuitive way he recognized the need for some additional, last-minute mischief to keep the pot boiling, to keep his rendezvous with doom on track.

Consider this mysterious incident, which occurred on the eve of the fateful final day:

Ken Rex showed up on the street in front of the house of Pete Ward, who was due to be the key witness against him at the bond-revocation hearing. He was on foot, with one of his women waiting in a backup truck at a distance down the street. He began to pace back and forth on the sidewalk, glaring at the house, as if he might be able to stare down the house the way he had once been able to stare down people.

He made no attempt to enter the house or to go into the yard. He didn't yell any threats or insults; he showed no hostile intentions except by the intensity of his stare. He just walked back and forth out there, looking.

A little later he went over to Gary Dowling's house and did the same thing.

What a curious sight that must have been—the legendary lord of the Nodaway night pacing back and forth in broad daylight, under a brutal July sun, like an inscrutable, solitary picket or like one of those back-and-forth plastic ducks in a shooting gallery. What in the world did he have in mind?

Was he just an old dinosaur eyeing extinction and tramping toward it? An over-the-hill bully strutting and fretting his last hour on an improbable stage, trying to prove himself one more time? Was he trying to show that he could still intimidate with just his ponderous physical presence and his famous stare?

117

Or was he trying to lure Ward out, as he had lured Romaine Henry?

He would have made an awfully easy target out there. One day nearly a year before, Ken Rex had paced the street in front of the Christian church, a submachine gun in one hand but the ammunition for it in the other. Pastor Tim Warren could have shot him then as easily as Ward could have shot him now. Had the tommy gun been just a prop intended even back then to spook the pastor into shooting him? The tommy gun on the street, like the recent bayonet in the tavern, was an unusual, attention-getting weapon. But Ken Rex hadn't been able to provoke anyone with his showy, scary weapons, so he seemed now to be trying an opposite approach, one that hinted at desperation and had in it almost the quality of beseeching. He was exposing himself, defenseless, in full daylight view of a sworn enemy.

But myth-sized events won't be rushed, and Ward, watching from inside his house, resisted any temptation he might have had to take up the challenge, while Ken Rex could do nothing more aggressive than pace back and forth on the street. What Ward saw was the same old Ken Rex, bolder than ever in his unrelenting campaign to intimidate and terrorize the town. That night Ward sat guard in the dark in his rocking chair in his front room. He sat there throughout the night with a pistol in his lap.

It would be Ken Rex's last stalk. Perhaps it was a final, forlorn attempt by an illiterate man to communicate something—perhaps a vain bid to escape a loudening bell that was pealing intolerably somewhere inside his brain.

By July 9, spirits were steady in Skidmore. The townspeople had counted off the days and sweated out the

nights, and were now gearing up for the hearing at
Bethany on the next day.

The tense wait was almost over, and nothing really terrible had happened. Optimism had begun to disperse
some of the apprehension and skepticism. Just one more
night and it would all be over.

If all went well, Ken Rex would be in jail tomorrow, his
bond revoked. He would stay in jail until the appeal of his
conviction was exhausted, and then he would go straight
to prison. It would be months before he got out again, and
even then things would never be the same.

There would be no more playing king of the hill and
lord of the night. Ken Rex would know that Skidmore
would never again tolerate his hooliganism, his ruthless
disregard of the community's cherished conventions. He
would be an ex-con, stigmatized, and he would behave
himself or Skidmore, having cuffed him once, would do it
again.

There was every reason to believe that all would go well
tomorrow. Pete Ward, backed by his sons and Dowling,
would be a match for McFadin's glibness, because Ward
and the others had truth on their side.

So there was hope—almost relish—in the conversations
that took place on the eve. Men came together in the cafe,
in the tavern, in the grocery store, on the street corners,
on the turnrows.

"You planning to make the trip to Bethany tomorrow?"

"Ain't everybody?"

"I wouldn't miss it for nothing."

"Been a long time coming, but it'll be worth it to see
'em put that shitass behind bars."

"Yeah. Fellow could get rich off it if he went about it

right. Set up a booth on the courthouse lawn and sell tickets to let folks peek through the window at the sorry son of a bitch."

"Be a line half a mile long."

"Yeah, and I'd be right at the front."

"You'd have to get there early to get ahead of me."

But a great bitterness was in store for Skidmore. Word came from Bethany by way of Maryville late that day: The hearing tomorrow had been postponed. Instead of July 10, it would be held on July 20.

Mayor Peter was among those who learned that evening of the bad tidings from Bethany. He got together with some of the other town leaders—those who had organized the Bethany caravan—and they mulled over the consequences of the postponement.

"We wanted to get together and discuss our options," the mayor said later. "If we had any."

They knew that the postponement would kill the town's morale. Timing had been the crucial element in the stand-up-and-be-counted movement. People had agreed to stick their necks out because they thought the issue would be settled quickly and conclusively. Now they would learn that the countdown wouldn't end tomorrow, after all. Their necks would be stuck out for *ten more days and nights*. With Ken Rex still on the prowl.

Ten days wasn't a long time, but in this case it might as well have been ten years.

The meeting of the town leaders was gloomy indeed. As one of them described it later, "It was on the order of, 'Your honor, I move that we count to three and all just say *shit* together.' "

But someone in the group came up with an idea. No one

could tell later whose idea it was, and maybe it dawned on them all at the same time.

"Why don't we get the prosecutor to come out and explain why he agreed to the postponement of the hearing? He owes it to us—"

That casual, sardonic remark changed everything. The men in the meeting began to kick the idea around, and the more they talked about it the better it sounded to them. Since so many people were already planning to gather the next morning at the Legion Hall for the caravan to Bethany, why not just tell them to come on, or let them come on, and invite Prosecutor Baird over to tell them in person just what was going on and why?

The idea was to turn the Legion Hall gathering into a town meeting. It would be an even more effective demonstration of Skidmore's commitment and concern than the trek to Bethany would have been. Nobody would have to wait ten days or drive seventy miles to stand up and be counted.

Such a meeting would show Prosecutor Baird, who *was* a politician after all, just how strong the sentiment against Ken Rex had become in this little corner of the Nodaway Empire. And maybe through this politician the message would get back to Maryville and shake up the indifferent courthouse clique.

For his part, Baird would be able to give Skidmore the firsthand, horse's-mouth dope on the reason for the bond-violation imbroglio and the status of the ongoing legal maneuvering over the Bowenkamp-shooting conviction. The explanations might quell some of the rumors and inflammatory gossip about what was going on with the lawyers and the courts.

Baird also should be able to give the townspeople some

reliable legal advice as to what community action they could possibly take to protect themselves and their peace of mind until such time as Ken Rex McElroy finally shook hands with the penitentiary warden.

As the prosecutor who had finally pinned a criminal conviction (meager as it was) on Ken Rex, Baird would be a walking-talking reminder that the system could work. He would be a symbol of hope, and Skidmore certainly needed that at this juncture.

So the word went out: Come on to the Legion Hall in the morning as planned. The caravan to Bethany was off, but something that might be even better was on.

Judgment Day

"I liked my town, my cornfields and the
home of my people. I fought for
them. . . . We took up the hatchet to
revenge injuries which my people could no
longer stand. That is why I fought. Now
the hatchet is buried."
                    —Black Hawk, spoken to
                    President Andrew Jackson

Out in the country, down a dusty road that snaked along
the old homestead grid, in a white-frame farmhouse at the
edge of a soybean field, the man lay alone in his bed in
predawn darkness, thinking. Or trying to think. The bell-
tormented thoughts weren't clear. They fought each other, murdered one another.

Something was in the air, and he knew what it was, but
he couldn't bring it up to the level of clear thought. Something was up, though, because it hadn't let him sleep a
wink.

He fought the impulse to get up and go into town. He fought it because the going-into-town hadn't helped these last few nights. A couple of times he had made himself look bad by trying to push the thing when it wasn't going to let itself be pushed. He hated them, all of them, for making him wait, for dragging it out.

He reached in the darkness for a cigarette and lit it. The flare of the lighter glinted on the field-trial trophies and the bayonet, and gleamed softly on the gunmetal and the polished gunstocks. For a moment he saw them in the lingering glow; he liked to look at them, just look at them, for they gave him an easiness. He flipped the lighter again and saw the objects clearly, but the easiness wouldn't stay.

He got up, pulled on his pants, and went out to the front porch. The night had been hot—too hot for him—and there wasn't much of a breeze even this early in the morning. He stood and looked out, trying to make no noise that would disturb the sleeping women and the kids.

The kids were on his mind. There was something he wanted to tell them, but what it was wasn't clear and he didn't know how. They were good kids, he was proud of that, and any son of a bitch that tried—

Something was definitely in the air. He knew what it was but it wouldn't come clear.

The dogs knew it too. He and the dogs always knew things that no one else knew. The dogs were restless, sensing him there on the porch. One of them had begun to growl when he first came out, and now he hushed it by leaning over and looking sternly at it.

He gazed off to the east, waiting for dawn. It had been a bad night, one of those hot summer nights that the farmers love, when they say you can actually hear the corn growing in the fields. He didn't give a damn about any corn, and he hated the summer heat. Since he had put on all the weight, the heat hurt him. The only remedy was beer. He could use a cold one now, even this early.

The crescent moon had set three hours before, but the night was bright with that summer luminescence which adds to the starlight the undissipated glower of the prolonged day. The dew was down, and the rolling Nodaway landscape was noisy with the chitter of a million night creatures. He waited for dawn, but the night was really his element. And those creatures had long been his unallegiant minions. They made a crazy noise at this hour before dawn. They too knew whatever it was that was in the air.

The man stood for a time on the porch under the wooden eagle, which, stopped in its flight, was nailed up over the portal in a state of permanent imperviousness. He stood looking off to the northwest, toward the town now. His thoughts wouldn't come clear. The night went to rawness in his mind, and he stood staring through the nothing toward the town.

Whatever was in the air was coming from that direction.

*

Lights came on before dawn in most of the Harry Truman–looking houses in and around Skidmore. Men had arranged to be away from their jobs, their businesses, their farms, but there were chores to be done before the morning rendezvous at the Legion Hall. Even those with no chores to do rose early—they were restless, impatient to get on with it.

JUDGMENT DAY

Last night had been hot and sticky, buggy and restless. Tossing and turning. Waiting for Ken Rex. This was the last night, the longest one, the most dreaded. All night there was nothing but the tossing and turning, the waiting, finally the drifting off to sleep just before dawn, when he didn't come.

Inside one of those lighted houses sat a solitary man, destined in this drama to be faceless and nameless—nothing more than an eye, a finger, and a brief racket. He had spent a sleepless night too, impatient for the break of Judgment Day. Inside this room too was the glint and gleam of weaponry. And an open book on the table gave a clue to what the man was thinking.

"How long, O Lord?" it asked. "How long wilt thou look on?"

A band of clouds had drifted up during the night from eastern Kansas, so the dawn was purple, promising some needed rain. But the rising sun got to the clouds before they could deliver their bounty. It sucked them dry and left the circular horizon as blue as the inside of a painted bell.

Birds arced down out of the wind and alit in the tall trees along Main Street. Some good lightning was needed to stir up the clouds, people thought as they came out of their houses. The birds chattered early today, as though the wind had made them afraid or blood-hungry.

There would be no rain on this day. It would be just another scorcher—ninety degrees and rising by noon-time.

Some of the country men came into town early—by seven—driving in from their farms out on the bituminous roads to Quitman and Maitland, to Graham and Fairfax. They stopped at Mom's Cafe, some of them, and began to learn about the postponement of the hearing over at Bethany.

JUDGMENT DAY

The town men already knew about the postponement, and also knew that the mayor and the banker and others were trying to get the prosecutor to come and talk to everybody. Inside the cafe, the men were getting antsy now. They talked, they grumbled. They would give that prosecutor a piece of their mind. They would make him understand just how it had been for them during these nights of waiting and wondering. They would make him understand just how much this postponement meant to them. They would grab him by his starched collar and shake some sense into him if they had to.

There was talk in the town of forming a citizens committee to keep watch on Ken Rex. So that if he tried to bother anybody, a whole crowd would swarm down on him like a pack of hounds on a vicious old coon. It sounded like a good idea. Maybe, they were hoping, they could get the details all worked out at the meeting this morning.

Other cars and pickups soon rolled into town. The news was spreading all over town.

"Postponed? You gotta be kidding. Till when?"

"Twentieth of the month. Week from Monday."

"Hell, that's another workday. I can't keep taking off for this thing."

"That's what the lawyer's counting on, more than likely. You know they strung old Bo along for nearly a year."

"Same old story then."

"What's the deal then? We just forget it this morning and go on back home?"

"Supposed to meet up at the Legion Hall here in a little while. Prosecutor's coming to tell us what's what. They're talking about getting up a citizens committee."

"What the hell *for?*"

"Don't ask me. I'm just here because I thought it would be fun to have my wife raped and my house burnt down in the middle of the night."

"A hanging committee would be more like it."

"I'll vote for that. You make the motion and I'll second it."

Even as the men of Skidmore gathered for the meeting, Mayor Peter and the other town leaders were still trying to get a speaker for it. They hadn't been able to get in touch with Prosecutor Baird the night before, and they failed again this morning.

"If we can't get Baird, let's get Estes."

"The sheriff? That guy?"

"He'll beat nothing."

So it was agreed. Banker Ken Hurner put through a call to Maryville, reached the sheriff's office, and after a wait, got Sheriff Estes to agree to come on over to Skidmore.

By eight o'clock Skidmore was bustling, and by nine there were so many people in town that it looked like it was Punkin Festival parade day. All the parking places were taken along the street where the Legion Hall looks across to the B&B Grocery, and there were more cars and pickups around the corner, fringing the stem of the T, scattered on down past D&G's, past Mom's Cafe, past the red depot with the blue boxcar sitting beside it.

Nearly a hundred people, all told, counting the women. Wary of getting the women involved, thinking about rolls of bologna and bitten-off nipples, most of the men left their women at home.

The knots of men gravitated up to the Legion Hall

from the cafe and the dinky little city hall. They milled around outside for a time, then gradually drifted inside, each newcomer digging himself out a folding chair and remarking favorably to the others on the size of the turn-out. By nine-thirty there were seventy-five or eighty men in the Legion Hall—a throng by Skidmore standards.

As the hall filled up, there was still grumbling about the postponement of the hearing. There was evidence of good feelings too—wisps of the kind of joviality you see at revival meetings, political gatherings, Punkin Festivals: a bit of joshing here, a clap on the back there, a chortle showing the candy-pink gums of new dentures. Those who had had doubts about getting involved in this business were relieved to find that they had so much company. They laughed a little. They were in the right place and maybe just a little proud of themselves because of it.

"Look who's here! What are you doing here, an old coward like you?"

"Oh, I'm lost."

"Look over there in the corner. I'm surprised that old skinflint would spend the gas money to get here."

"Hell, he's the richest man in Nodaway County. Got enough money to burn a wet mule."

This kind of banter masked some of the concern, the frustration, the bitterness over Ken Rex's having wriggled free once again. It masked some of the impatience to get on with the task of squelching Ken Rex once and for all.

But it didn't mask it very well. These men hadn't come here for the hell of it. They had come to hear somebody say: "Damn all this worrying and wondering and pussy-footing around. This is what we've got to do. So let's do it."

129

The mayor and the banker and some of the other leaders came in finally. Pete Ward moved to the front of the rostrum and took the role of emcee, or ringmaster, long enough to get everyone's attention and convey the news formally:

"For those of you who haven't already heard," Ward said, "the hearing over at Bethany has been postponed till the twentieth of the month."

"What?" a voice grumbled from the back of the room. "How the hell did he do that?"

"Don't know," one of the leaders answered blandly.

"Ken Rex's lawyer's got him a delay of ten more days," Ward said, and then sort of shrugged.

The meeting began to break down into chatter. Toward the back of the hall, the men were talking among themselves. Up front, the leaders spoke about the need to keep the momentum of this stand-up-and-be-counted movement going. The ten-day delay was a bitter pill all right, they said, but Ken Rex would be no match for this many good men sticking together and standing up for one another.

"Other crime watches have worked. Why shouldn't ours?"

It was true. Other towns around had resorted to citizen committees, and they had proved effective in keeping troublemakers in line. No reason why Skidmore couldn't do that, too, with this many concerned citizens ready to do their part. But it had to be done right, the mayor kept saying. They would have to avoid any step that might jeopardize the pending court action against Ken Rex.

And to make sure that they didn't do the wrong thing, Sheriff Estes was on his way over from Maryville to advise them on how they should proceed.

130

"The sheriff? I thought the prosecutor was coming."

"No."

"Why not? He's the one that let 'em get by with postponing this hearing today."

"Well, the prosecutor couldn't make it."

"I just bet he couldn't."

"The sheriff's the one we'll have to coordinate this thing with anyway. Let's hear him out. I think he'll work with us."

"How's he gonna find his way over here? Did one of you guys send him a map?"

In the back of the hall, two of the men who had talked earlier in the cafe looked at each other. One of them leaned over and said, "S.O.S.," and the other nodded disconsolately and muttered, "Yeah, same old shit."

The meeting had degenerated into conversational buzzing as the men talked among themselves, commenting skeptically and bitingly on what was going on. But then, a few minutes later, the door to the hall opened, the lawman walked in, and everyone grew silent. It was almost ten.

Like Prosecutor Baird, Mayor Peter, and Pastor Tim Warren, Sheriff Estes was a young man in his twenties. Stocky and muscular, with light curly hair that was beginning to thin on top, he was a serious young fellow who gave the impression of wanting to do right by people. He was obviously a rising star in Nodaway County politics, but he had been sheriff only a few months and had been a deputy for four years before that, and these were precisely the years during which Skidmore had become disillusioned with county law enforcement, and convinced that the sheriff's department was woefully overmatched by

Ken Rex McElroy. Because of this situation, and because he could sense the townspeople's exasperation, Estes appeared a little nervous and ill at ease. And the same sentiment could be read in all the men's eyes: He was the wrong man at the wrong place at the wrong time.

He stood at the front of the hall, conferring with some of the town leaders; they were filling him in on the discussion so far about the possibility of forming a crime-watch committee in Skidmore, and he was nodding his head. He agreed to tell the crowd what he knew about the concept, and to answer their questions about its local application.

Now Mayor Peter and the others were encouraged. Maybe a productive brainstorming session would follow. As soon as Estes began to speak, the men in the hall could tell he was nervous but trying not to show it. He didn't smile, didn't indulge in any good-natured small talk; he made no attempt to break the official mood that his presence had brought to the meeting.

He started making recommendations—the conventional stuff, which seemed dragged out a little. The men in the hall leaned back and began to lose themselves in their own thoughts. At the end of his little speech, the sheriff suggested that the men of Skidmore establish something he called "a standing Ken Rex alert," in order to keep an eye on his every move while he was still in circulation and let the town and the authorities know of any suspicious activities they saw him engaging in.

Mayor Peter asked the first question. Couldn't it be considered harassment, he asked, to follow a man around, shadowing his every move?

Just following someone around was perfectly legal, the sheriff replied, so long as it was done peacefully and no trespassing was committed.

Then someone in the crowd asked Estes what *he* planned to do to keep Ken Rex under control during the coming days and nights.

"Ain't it your responsibility to keep law and order in Nodaway County, Sheriff? Wasn't that what you were elected to do?"

That triggered a spate of similar questions. Wasn't the sheriff sloughing off his duty by putting the full burden of keeping the peace on the citizens of Skidmore? Had he considered assigning a deputy to patrol in and around Skidmore at night until Ken Rex was safely behind bars? Where had the law been when Ken Rex was out running wild?

The sheriff had walked into a hornet's nest. Standing erect, he fielded the questions and took a little time before giving simple, logical, and unemotional replies. His voice was controlled, his words skillful. He did not lose patience as he explained the handicaps he was working under.

Most of the men in the hall had stopped paying attention to him because they had heard all the explanations and excuses before. They had come to the meeting ready to *do* something about Ken Rex, something decisive and conclusive. They had come thinking they had Ken Rex on the run, on his way to jail, and they were ready to do their part to see this wearing business through to a satisfactory end.

But it was clear from the start that all this meeting had going for itself was this empty crime-watch notion. They had no stomach for it.

"This isn't a proposal for action," someone mumbled.

Several people nodded agreement. It was a proposal for *reaction*. It would require them to spend their time anticipating how Ken Rex would spend his time. They would have to arrange their lives around him. Ken Rex would still be calling the shots, perhaps literally, on his terms, according to his schedule.

"What good is it going to do?"

And that was a good question, too, one that the sheriff and the leaders up front would have a hard time with. How effective could a Skidmore crime watch be, really? What protection would it offer against the whispered midnight threat, the rattlesnake in the mailbox, the shotgun suddenly thrust out of the shadows into somebody's gut? Who could tell, when the McElroy convoy roared through the darkness, whether Ken Rex was really in one of the pickups? Ernest Bowenkamp was sitting in this meeting listening and trying not to show his frustration. Would following Ken Rex around, dogging his movements, have prevented what happened to old Bo? Romaine Henry was sitting over at the side of the hall. Keeping an eye on Ken Rex had put Romaine through the worst ordeal of his life.

The men in the audience couldn't tell the sheriff what they were thinking. There were no proper words. How could you convey that the Nodaway nights were Ken Rex's medium, not theirs. When Ken Rex wrapped himself in the small-hours darkness, he was more than just a basset-eyed fat man. He was a criminal legend that this lawman refused to know. And simple vigilance would be no match for a legend—no more than this young sheriff was, standing up there prating away.

The meeting was drifting out of focus, trailing off into irrelevancy, but it was suddenly brought back into sharp resolution by a question that came from the back of the hall. There was a pause. The question was so pointed that the whole hall seemed to draw one long breath.

134

JUDGMENT DAY

"What does the son of a bitch have to do before one of us could just go out and kill him?"

No one could say who asked it. Around the dim old hall the faces of the men turned grim. Any one of them might have asked the question. *All* of them had asked it, really, even if only one person had given it voice. All of them had asked it, as nearly all people everywhere have asked it at one time or another.

The men in the hall knew there had been talk around Skidmore for years about how it would simplify matters if somebody would catch Ken Rex on a back road some night and just shoot him dead. Mostly that talk had been saloon muttering—wishful fantasy paroled up to the level of slurred braggadocio by one too many beers. Or it had been a way of concluding somber conversations on a not-so-dreary note: When the men were sitting around talking over coffee, over a beer, or on a turnrow, talking about Ken Rex's latest outrage, saying what was Skidmore ever going to do about that guy, shaking their heads, then someone saying in a flippant way with a smile that meant he wasn't speaking seriously: "Well, somebody ought to just take the son of a bitch out and shoot him."

It was a fantasy they had all shared. But in recent days something had been in the air, something pertaining to this, but different and ominous, something elusive, vague. And the flippant remark about killing had died in the throat unspoken, and the one beer too many had no longer been enough.

Now the question had been brought out into the open.

The sheriff couldn't answer it. Justifiable homicide is a tricky legal concept that lawmen have enough trouble contending with *after* the fact. All Estes could do was review some of the murky precedents, and the fact that he was trying to give an answer to the question was lost on

135

the men in the hall now. Because the question wasn't addressed to him. It wasn't addressed to anybody—except maybe to God. And it was simply raised, as if it had emanated from the collective mind of the meeting. Once raised, it eclipsed all other questions—the ones that had already been asked and the ones that hadn't; it made all the other questions seem impotent, pointless, and trivial.

After handling the question as best he could, the sheriff said he had to get back to his office in Maryville.

The meeting's organizers thanked him for coming out. One or two of them followed him to the door.

He left quickly.

It was ten-thirty by now and some of the men at the meeting began to drift out of the Legion Hall. That hanging question, coupled with the sheriff's departure, made it seem pointless to stay. Romaine Henry left and went home. Ernest Bowenkamp came up the aisle and went out without a word; he was on his way back to work at the B&B Grocery. A few other men got up and moved toward the door.

But most of the men stayed, talking among themselves, although the meeting lost any semblance of organization. Yet something seemed to hold the men there. Whatever had been in the air—a vague sense of expectancy—still hadn't dissipated.

The meeting might have broken up completely within a few minutes, but then one of the men who had left minutes earlier came huffing excitedly back across the dusty street and reentered the Legion Hall. He poked his head through the door and said:

"Ken Rex's in town! He's down at D&G's with Trena right now."

There was a brief silence, followed by a general hubbub. They had expected him the night before, roaring around and raising hell, but what was he doing here now, skulking about town at midmorning?

A few men got up and ventured out to see for themselves. They walked to the corner and saw that indeed the big brown pickup with the mud flaps was parked down in front of the tavern.

The commotion gave a few others—the reluctant ones—the chance to slip discreetly away, one nudging another with an elbow and saying in a low tone: "Let's get out of here. You see what's happened. He's got wind of this meeting and he's come in to see who all's involved. Sees my truck out there, no telling what might happen to my wife and daughter."

"Yeah, I was against this thing from the start anyhow."

Back in the hall, one man had leaned forward in a silent rage as word came that Ken Rex was in their midst. He seized the moment now to detach himself from the crowd. He was the nameless and faceless one, and now he had become the bloody-minded one. His question—how long, O Lord?—had been answered as if by Providence. Ken Rex was here, now. That was the answer.

Those who had gone to look around the corner now returned.

"Yeah, he's down there, all right."

"He's a nervy bastard, I'll say that for him."

Mayor Peter came up to the front of the crowd then. He had realized during the interval that here was an almost miraculous opportunity to salvage the meeting and to reaffirm the crime-watch notion. The notion had seemed utterly lost just a few minutes before—lost to indifference and scorn—but here was a chance to put it into action and show just how effective it could be.

"All right," Steve Peter said, "the sheriff said we ought to keep an eye on him. Let's go keep an eye on him."

JUDGMENT DAY

The mood of the men, which had gone from ambivalence to optimism to gloom, now abruptly changed to enthusiasm. You could feel it through the musty little hall, recharging and becoming electric.

Skidmore suddenly had come together and assumed the shape of the opposing character in the drama the fates had decreed. It would have its showdown, and it wouldn't have to wait ten days or ten years for it. It wouldn't have to trudge all the way to Bethany, and it wouldn't have to adopt the meek pose of an obscure character sitting dumbly through a boring and confounding court hearing.

"Hell, what are we waiting for?"

"Let's go!"

"Damn right!"

They made their plan almost without discussion. They didn't need to hash it out because they were a single-minded character, a mind-set. They were Skidmore.

And Skidmore would march over to the tavern and give Ken Rex a look at a real opponent. They would buy beers for one another and toast those four witnesses right under Ken Rex's nose. They would mirror that evil-eye stare with a hundred and twenty eyes and see if that didn't melt him on the spot.

"We're going to *watch* him, remember," one of the leaders cautioned. "Don't anybody do anything rash."

The caution wasn't necessary. Skidmore was a character now and it knew what to do. The drama was on track.

Skidmore surged toward the door and poured out onto the bright street, anxious to get on with it.

*

The men crossed the street and then rounded the corner where the bank rests in the left armpit of the T-shaped intersection. The handful of women who work in the bank watched them through the window as they passed in front of the bank and then alongside, across the street from the post office nestled in the looming weathered storefront.

There were other women in the bank watching them too—women who had come into town with their husbands and who had entered the bank lobby to get out of the July heat, waiting for the big meeting to adjourn.

The women watched the men pass and felt whatever it was that was in the air.

The men who were now Skidmore didn't walk fast, but they didn't amble either. Four or five abreast, they filled the space between the street-front buildings and the vehicles parked on an angle along the stem of the T, many men moving as one, as the buffalo had moved as one.

You could hear the tramping of their feet.

As that tramp tramp tramp grew to the dimensions and proportions of myth, the bloody-minded one quietly peeled away from the group. He stopped behind one of the vehicles and watched Skidmore tramp away to play its part. He crouched there a moment, readying his insides so that he would be able to play his own.

Inside the tavern, you could hear the coming of Skidmore, its tramping like the cadence of some wayward battalion. Ken Rex heard it and knew what it meant; he had heard it before in the darkness of his soul and had been waiting for it.

A brief bottleneck developed at the tavern's narrow door as the main body of men arrived. The mayor went in, and then the others began quickly to duck in behind him, not pausing to think about it. The ones bringing up the rear shuffled nervously, waiting their turn to enter.

JUDGMENT DAY

A defector at the last instant scuttled quickly away, back up the street toward the bank, but he wasn't the bloody-minded one, because the bloody-minded one, if he had ever been with this crowd, would never have come so conspicuously far with them.

Ken Rex stood down at the far end of the bar in his customary place, his woman at his side. As Skidmore filed in, man after man, Ken Rex moved a little back from the bar, out in the open, and watched. The woman watched him watching the others, and must have wondered what it was he saw that she didn't, what was going on, what had brought them both here today.

Red Smith, the bartender, moved up the bar to greet some of the first ranks. Red wasn't himself today; he wasn't jovial and talkative as usual. The first men started ordering beers all around. The bartender lined up a row of mugs at the tap.

Something was in the air.

Skidmore kept coming. It was a record crowd for D&G's—certainly a record morning crowd. Not even at the height of the Punkin Festival had the place been so jammed. Bigger inside than it looks from the street, the tavern allowed the overflow to fan out around the bar, the service tables, the pool tables, the Ping-Pong table, the pinball machine—all the way back to the unplugged juke-box.

Ken Rex moved back up to the bar. He still faced the front where Skidmore was bunching. The woman leaned over and whispered something to him, but he seemed to pay no mind to it. He didn't deign to notice the men; he seemed to look beyond them, and Skidmore read that as an early advantage.

He had stared down some of these same men before in this place, wilted them with that cold stare until they

140

slouched away. But not now. He knew better than to try.

The men sipped their beer, clapped one another on the back, offered their toasts—ignoring him as pointedly as he was ignoring them.

"Let him wonder," Skidmore said to itself. Let him think that their meeting had been a rousing success, that they had come up with a dandy strategy for foiling him and were so confident about it that they had come to celebrate.

Laughing, joking, buying rounds, they acted like men without a worry in the world. They were a force.

Ken Rex showed them nothing, but they felt him testing them just the same. He could read them without looking, and they sensed the silent scan. They knew that if one of them showed the smallest trace of irresolution, the subtlest suggestion of failure of nerve, he would pick up on it and read it right on through the rest of them, through this character Skidmore, like a seismologist reading a geological fault.

He waited.

Skidmore kept up its show.

Still he waited, and still Skidmore filled every wavelength with the same message: "We'll stay here all day if that's what it takes to convince you. We'll stay here till hell freezes over."

He waited until he was sure, and then he did something he had never done in this place, his favorite haunt, the headquarters of his enduring and inscrutable campaign. He signaled Red Smith and told him he wanted a six-pack of beer to go.

A barkeep makes his reputation by knowing his customers—their drinking habits and peculiarities. Red Smith knew Ken Rex never ordered beer to go.

141

"To go?"

"Yeah. And I need a package of Rolaids too."

The showdown was over, Skidmore knew. But the men kept up their banter as Ken Rex steered Trena toward the door. The noise in the place could not dull the tension each man felt as the big man paced by.

The two of them maneuvered past the young mayor, and as they did, Ken Rex glanced directly into Steve Peter's eyes and gave him a parting nod.

The mayor wondered what the nod meant; he would wonder about it long afterward. Maybe it was a deferential nod, as if to say, "All right, you convinced me. Even if it was just a big bluff, it was a damn good one." Or it might have been a supercilious one, as if to say, "You think you've done it, but you haven't. It'll take a lot more than this." Or it might have meant nothing more than just, "Hello and goodbye, sorry things didn't work out so the two of us could have got to know one another."

When Ken Rex emerged from the dark little tavern into the dazzling July sunlight, he squinted and paused. It was then that the thought must have struck him for the first time that he had nowhere to go.

If he left here now, he could never return as the man he had been, as the only man he had ever wanted to be. He had lost his power, his credibility, his reputation, and there was nowhere he could go to get these things back. There was nowhere he could go to forget about them or learn to live without them.

He had nowhere to go.

Everywhere now was prison.

Inside the tavern, Skidmore exulted for a moment, not noisily but inwardly. To each man the triumph meant something different—the vanquishing of his own private demon of self-doubt. Some swapped smiles and raised their eyebrows in delight. Some thought silently about what had happened and what it might mean. It was a moment to savor, to guzzle down the glasses of beer that they had only sipped at before.

But the struggle wasn't over yet, and it was no time to gloat. They would have to clinch the victory by pressing the offensive. They had shown Ken Rex where they stood, whose side they were on, but they hadn't shown him enough. They hadn't shown him that they intended to bedevil him as he had bedeviled them—that they intended to watch him, follow him, dog his every move until he was behind bars. And if he managed again to avoid imprisonment, they would *still* hound him—until he gave up trying, until he wouldn't dare show his face again where decent people gathered.

No one had to tell Skidmore to follow Ken Rex out.

The mayor went first and the others began to fall in behind him.

The street was abnormally quiet, like on a Sunday. There were none of the workaday sounds and sights of Skidmore—no traffic, no one to be seen up and down the street. The mockingbird was no longer purling up by the Methodist church. Such an eerie hush steals across the prairie sometimes, easing up over the glacial rolls and settling over the swales like dusk or fog. But this one was so profound that there was still a suggestion in the air of the tramping of men's feet a half hour before. Or a half century before. Or a century and a half.

The fierce July sun had moved high up over the stem of the T, and the radiated heat had begun to undulate up from the pavement and from the hoods and tops of cars and pickups parked along both sides of the street. Skidmore, as Ken Rex stood looking at it, shimmered like a mirage.

The brown Chevy pickup was parked at a slight angle directly in front of D&G's. Trena was already climbing in on the passenger side when Mayor Peter and the others started coming out the tavern door. Ken Rex broke his reverie and walked around the front of the truck and got in on the driver's side.

Skidmore continued to squeeze out of the tavern, a few men at a time—ten, fifteen, twenty. They collected near the right front fender of the pickup. As their ranks deepened, they fanned out as they had done in the bar, so that the group arced a few feet from the truck, from the right headlight to the right door handle. They all had their eyes on Ken Rex. They wore a common expression—the old Ken Rex stare, proliferated and turned back on him.

More of them were still coming out of the tavern.

*

In the cab of the pickup, the woman was suddenly alarmed. She was saying something to Ken Rex, but he didn't seem to hear. Or it was as though he had heard before what she was saying now, and knew that what she was saying didn't matter. He reached forward to the ignition, put his thumb and forefinger on the key, but didn't turn it.

Something was wrong. This was the time, and yet the sound of the bells wouldn't clarify. He had nowhere to go.

The woman was frantic now, but he didn't turn the key.

144

JUDGMENT DAY

Seconds thumped by like heartbeats, and still he couldn't will his hand to turn the key.

He sat, leaning forward over the steering wheel, gazing absently into the vacuum of unsounding bells, his thumb and forefinger unmoving on the key.

It was all over, just as he had sensed that it would be, and yet it wasn't over. Something had been in the air, and he had read it as no one else could. What he had read was that this moment would be his, not theirs. It would be the moment of his supreme vindication—the moment he had fought and thieved and drunk and fucked and bullied and terrorized his way toward ever since those days of boyhood humiliations, of blowing dust and bumpkin squalor. The moment that would permanently secure his power over this place which he hated to love and loved to hate and which he could never get away from. The moment when the failing influence of a man would be transmuted into the enduring influence of a legend.

That moment had come, and it wouldn't come again. He had prepared for it, but now the bells wouldn't clarify it, and as it slipped away he didn't know what to do. He had nowhere to go. The next minutes, the next years, were a void in which the only man he had ever wanted to be could not be. He was mystified. He was blank as the moment thumped irretrievably away, and his thumb and forefinger remained unmoving on the meaningless ignition key.

"They've got a gun . . . hurry—"

The myth will determine what it was the woman saw and exactly what she said or screamed. This much is certain: She was frantic. She sensed the disaster hurtling toward the cab of the pickup with great force and velocity.

But her warning or plea was sucked away into that vacuum of unringing bells as he sat, unheeding, blank, his thumb and forefinger still motionless on the ignition key.

Skidmore flanging the truck was a solemn tableau inside the moment, an expressionless group portrait that might at any second grain away to daguerreotype, fifty or a hundred or a hundred and fifty years old.

The moment seemed to go on forever, like rubber stretched tauter and tauter, elongated, and unbearable, until finally the shot:

Ka-WHOW!

The shot shattered the moment, and its reverberations thundered back and forth between the buildings down the street, riving the abnormal silence and transfixing the characters of the drama with the sheer force of the sound.

The first shot shattered the rear glass and whined on off down the stem of the T.

But before its echoes could die or even begin to fade—before the rift in the hush could close again, before the man and woman in the pickup or the men standing beside it could react—a second shot came roaring down the street, a monstrosity of sound that blottered the *thunk* and *clink* as the slug tore through his head and smashed on through the glass of the window beside him.

Now the woman's screams were released into the tormented air. Two more shots muscled violently through the tumult. Men yelled, pushing one another down hard to the sidewalk and pavement around the truck.

Ken Rex slumped forward. At last he had moved. The moment had been his after all, and now he could pass over into legend.

Aftermath

> We are all in it! Every sin is the result of a
> collaboration.
> > —from "The Blue Hotel"
> > by Stephen Crane

The dying echoes of the gunfire yielded to a momentary
clamor of sounds alien to the Skidmore street: muffled
shouts, the urgent but clumsy sound of many men throwing themselves down on hard pavement, a furious gyra-
tion of birds winging up from the tall trees on the little
town square, the scream and piercing wail of the one
woman on the scene—all blending into a strange aleatory
music, which, in Skidmore's reliving of the event in recur-
rent dreams, would become the legend's theme or
score.

If there had been a town clock working, it would have
just begun tolling the eleventh hour.

JUDGMENT DAY

Then the calm that had held the street only moments earlier washed back, smoothing over the disturbance. Whatever had been in the air before, agitating it, was now gone. A thin streamer of gun smoke drifted lazily along the street. Time held its breath, suspended, while the killer walked briskly away.

Now the men were standing up, moving cautiously toward the truck. The door to the tavern creaked open and others came out slowly, and they all formed a crescent, closing in on the vehicle, peering mutely. One of them, with help from another, and then another, got the woman away from the truck—having to hold her back from the horror—and shepherded her up to the bank at the end of the street.

Soon more men were gathered around the pickup. Three young boys who had been hiding down the alley behind the grocery store now made bold to come and see. They wormed in among the men who were gazing into the truck.

It was of these men standing mute around the truck that the fact finders would ask the questions that only the myth will answer. Who among them knew beforehand that this killing was in the works? Who among them, before they belly-flopped to the street or after they rose again, saw the killer and recognized him? Were any or all of them involved in a conspiracy to perpetrate this murder or to shield the person who pulled the trigger? To this day not one of the men has ever offered a clue to these questions.

What were their thoughts as they stood gawking into the truck? In the weeks and months to come, not one of them would ever say that he was appalled or remorseful.

AFTERMATH

"Nobody was heartbroken."

"Whoever did it did the whole town a favor."

"Nobody could say he didn't have it coming."

"Justice was done."

The comments were uniformly unrepentant, and Skidmore's stubborn refusal to play the contrition game became a big issue when the story made its way back through the gateway to the rest of the world.

If Skidmore had been more savvy about the ways of American politics and journalism, it would have done a lot of deploring and expressing of shock. Because if the people close to such a scene as this don't deplore adequately and express adequate shock, then opportunistic commentators and politicians, in a kind of conditioned response, will fill the breach. Stories like the Skidmore murder, with their almost unlimited deploring-and-expressing-shock potential, are hard to come by. But Skidmore was innocent of that kind of cynicism, and it felt no hypocritical urge to pretend to be horrified by what it saw in that pickup truck.

The cryptic comments the men made after they'd had days and weeks to look back on the event will have to suffice to guide the myth, but will never really reveal the men's thoughts as they gazed at the blasted remains of their old nemesis. Those comments show no remorse, but neither do they show any rejoicing, nor even any real satisfaction. They suggest that what those men thought when they stood there looking, just looking, was nothing.

Nothing at all.

The drama in which they were one of the two main characters had been building for years. The tension had been cresting for ten anxious days and nights. The men's emotions had gone up and down like the landscape, from rolls of enthusiasm to sudden swales of dejection. Just a moment before, they had scored what seemed a decisive triumph, which had, in a twinkling, as quick as a shot, transformed the whole experience into tragedy. The passion of that long drama, with all its twists and turns, was still so fresh that they couldn't even think, "Well, it's finally over." Not yet.

They just looked, astonished. In their fantasies they had many times pictured Ken Rex shot dead, so they didn't recoil now from the actualization of their long-held wishes. They felt no savage delight and no civilized revulsion, or maybe they felt both, but they thought nothing. No gorge rose, no one spat toward the dead man, no one grieved.

They just looked.

Then one, and soon another, turned to walk away. Then the others, as if waking from a reverie or trance, unspeaking, melted away. Within a minute or two the whole street was deserted. A slight breeze stirred then, taking with it the lingering pungent pall.

The last peal of the clock, if there had been a clock, would have sounded far out over the corn—as far out as that frame house where the man had heard a different gonging early that morning. The stillness that claimed the empty street was only a distant cousin of the earlier calm. It seemed almost scripted, an invitation to draw back, to pull one's perspective up and away and view the scene as an old hawk would have—to see it as a mindless pageant played out on this land as the result of the visitation of an old curse which touched down here for an inconsequential moment and then moved on.

Only Ken Rex was left, and he would be there for an hour yet, drawing flies, before they came to haul the dead bulk of him away.

He was quite a mess. The bullets had torn out bone and brains and blood in a great spew, disintegrating his chin and nose and mouth, leaving only the shell of a forehead and the eyes intact—the eyes that might have seen the tilt of the weapon for a split second in the rearview mirror, but at the stasis instantly pitched backward in the skull and then came forward to stare grotesquely down again at the most curious of all last focuses, the ignition key. Ken Rex's face had exploded, and a viscous gush had sucked the breath and vital humors out of him. He had trembled once, then flopped awkwardly forward to drape the wheel.

That's where they found him, an hour later, on a deserted street, under the noonday sun. He was in his final place, as if he had chosen to remain there forever. Even as he slumped there, his strong will seemed to continue, or at least the penetrating eyes seemed to go on narrowing and striking to the bone.

He's still there, too.

Skidmore thought it was shed of him, after letting him sit for an hour in the glass and gore, but it wasn't.

Maryville thought it was shed of him two months later, when the grand jury wrapped up its investigation, but it wasn't.

The rest of us thought we could be shed of him if we could just nail down the salient facts (that's how we shoo away the disquieting mysteries of life), but the facts here were quicksilver; they wheeled and danced like a Sac-Fox shaman's fireball. And after all the official and unofficial fact-finding field trips into Skidmore, Ken Rex was still there in his shot-up pickup truck, dead as hell and pressing the question:

What does it mean?

Trena had some disturbing things to say about what happened during that hour while her man sat festering on the deserted street.

When they got her into the bank, she said she told the woman there, "You didn't have to do him that way." And she said they told her it had to be done, that there was no other way. Trena portrayed the women as huddling there in the bank, aware beforehand that the murder would occur, and condoning it afterward.

She also said she telephoned a relative to come to the bank and take her home, and she said the relative found the roads to Skidmore blocked by men who wouldn't let traffic into town.

Such vague charges helped to fuel the idea that the murder had been a vigilante killing—a modern-day lynching. That idea was what brought newsmen streaming into Skidmore during the ensuing days and weeks and months, fanning enormous interest in the case across the country and even abroad, and it eventually lured the FBI up from Kansas City to investigate the possibility of a conspiracy.

There were certainly intimations of a lynching, even if there was no hard evidence. The men of Skidmore had gathered at the Legion Hall that morning to consider what action they might take as a group against Ken Rex. They had made no secret of their hostility and impatience. There was open, if hypothetical, talk of shooting Ken Rex. Later the men converged on Ken Rex in a deliberate confrontation. Anywhere from twenty to forty of them followed Ken Rex out to the street, watched him die, left the scene, and didn't notify the authorities. Furthermore, they gave absolutely no helpful information to the investigators and expressed no sorrow over what had happened. The conclusion seems inevitable.

Except for two details.

One is that the men at the meeting in the Legion Hall couldn't have known that Ken Rex would be in town that morning. If they hatched a murder plot against him, they did it in the very few minutes between the time someone brought the news of Ken Rex's presence in town and the time they left the hall together. Getting that many people to agree to *anything* in so short a span of time is an organizational improbability, as anyone who has ever chaired a committee will readily avow, and it is even more so if the proposal is for complicity in a cold-blooded murder.

Mobs have been known to commit spontaneous atrocities, though. But then there is a second detail. Which is this: At the moment Ken Rex was shot, those men who had followed him out of the tavern were standing only a few feet out of the line of fire. A rifle bullet deflecting or ricocheting off that truck could easily have killed any one of them. An inopportune nervous twitch or even a hiccup by the gunman could have bagged three or four. Those still in the tavern weren't safe either—not with a high-powered rifle popping in their general direction. It's foolish to think that all these men would have been so bold or would have taken such an unnecessary risk.

Anyone inclined to believe the lynching theory must

153

remember that the men of Skidmore didn't go dragging Ken Rex out, didn't nail him down or burn him. *He came to them.*

But a conspiracy of silence after the murder, an unspoken communal agreement to conceal the killer's identity—now that's another matter.

It's possible, with all the vehicles parked along the stem of the T that morning, that the killer managed his bloody task unseen. When the men of Skidmore came out of the tavern, they were looking at Ken Rex and only Ken Rex. They were watching him intently, not casually, with a purposeful concentration that might have kept them from being distracted by any movement the killer made up there on the corner. When the shooting started, the men hit the pavement. After the shooting stopped, the grotesque spectacle in the pickup compelled their attention long enough for the killer to walk away undetected.

Possible.

But anyone who has spent time in the community will come away with the sense that most of the townspeople know, all right, who the killer is. And one gets the impression that those who don't know have deliberately avoided finding out; the knowledge would be a burden they'd rather not have to live with. Nobody in Skidmore will flat out tell you any of these things, but they can be picked up from many small intangible signs. The look that comes into the eyes of some of the people when you broach the subject of whodunit, for instance—a quick gaze into nowhere, reflective and not at all troubled, as if they are picturing the scene again, seeing the killer at his killing, and reviewing all the reasons and excuses for keeping the matter secret. And also telltale are the comments which one knows by a sixth sense mean the opposite of what is said, as well as the comments which, if one hangs around long enough, one begins to realize are intended to send reporters and other nosy fact finders off on wild-goose chases.

And also this: Skidmore isn't New York or Kansas City or even St. Joseph, and in some ways it's as far away from Maryville as the buffalo. It's conceivable that a killer could go into any of those places and gun somebody down in broad daylight with a lot of people on the scene, and still completely escape identification. But it isn't conceivable that that could happen in Skidmore, Missouri, U.S.A.

The very small towns of America—the old-fashioned ones where everybody knows everybody else, and everybody knows everything that happens because nothing much ever does—just don't let an event like this spectacular murder happen anonymously. So somebody in Skidmore is bound to have seen something. Somebody is bound to have seen enough to know, and it wouldn't have been long before everyone who wanted to know did know. Can anyone imagine that Skidmore, after that phenomenal struggle against Ken Rex, would have been content to let the thing end without even knowing who it was that ended it?

The investigators took it for granted after a while that Skidmore was covering for somebody, and the question they pursued was *who.* Who in Skidmore (whose whereabouts at the time of the shooting were disputable) could command such amazing community allegiance? It's an interesting question, and when one considers how a community like Skidmore defines its ultimate values, the list of suspects narrows down quickly.

The mystery deepens when the question being asked is *why.* Why would a town want to cover for a murderer? It may not only be because the killer might have been a person who exerted great moral influence in the community—an authority beyond the reach of worldly judgment. And it may not only be because the community approved of the murder, considered it just.

It may also be because Skidmore realized that identifying the killer would trivialize the killing. If the killer had been fingered, booked, charged, and duly prosecuted, the killing would have represented nothing more than just another grubby murder. Murders happen every day. Of course, this would have been Skidmore's first murder ever, but so what? It might have rated a small headline, buried on an inside page in the St. Joe newspaper or even the state edition of the *Kansas City Star:*

SUSPECT IS CHARGED

IN NODAWAY SLAYING

However much that unwritten headline would have pleased the fact finders and the courthouse keepers of justice, it also would have left the drama of the great struggle between Ken Rex and Skidmore forever hanging. Skidmore would have won by default in the bottom of the ninth with the score tied or it would have lost by default. Ken Rex might not be around to intimidate the town again, but Skidmore would never have the satisfaction of refusing to let him.

What happened was charged with triumph and tragedy. Out of guilt, out of pride, out of a human aversion to absurdity, Skidmore needed to share in the credit or the blame for Ken Rex's death. If Skidmore had permitted either of the questions, whodunit and why, to be answered easily, it never could have come up with a tolerable answer to its own question, the only one that really mattered: What did it mean?

AFTERMATH

That question was to get lost and ignored as the courthouse crowd at Maryville went through the self-satisfied and self-serving motions of a routine disposition of the case.

*

Just past noon, the frantic rush of an ambulance out on County Road V alerted the countryside that something bad had happened in Skidmore. From as far out as White Cloud Creek the grimalkin mewl of the coming siren could be heard.

A county patrol car led the ambulance into town. Both vehicles slowed down as they passed the Methodist church and approached the town's little business district just ahead. The siren ceased. There was a strange hush over everything, so that one could hear the gentle sway of the wind in the tall old maples along main street.

An ambulance's squealing siren usually brings folks out of their houses, but that did not happen today. Not a soul was moving along the street. The ambulance and patrol car slowed down even more. Neither the men in the ambulance nor the deputy knew what to expect. They had been told only that a shooting had occurred in front of D&G's tavern. No one in Skidmore had notified the authorities of the shooting; no one called for an ambulance or a hearse. News of the shooting had reached the sheriff's office through the funeral home in Maryville—a lawyer in Kansas City had called in to say that someone had been shot, possibly even killed, in downtown Skidmore.

The ambulance and the patrol car went at a crawl now. The drivers were amazed to see that on this workday summer noon hour there was only one vehicle on the whole street—a brown Chevrolet pickup up there by the tavern. The ambulance drew alongside it and the attendants got out. The patrol car wheeled around, partially blocking the street.

There was a dreamlike quality to the scene as the ambulance attendants peered at the contorted corpse and then quickly looked away, surveying the silent street, which looked like it might have been deserted for a century.

Deputy Jim Kish, a sheriff's department investigator, emerged from the patrol car and stood out in the street. He raised his hand to stop a car approaching from the direction of Maryville—a car which seemed momentarily as intrusive in this dreamlike place of abandonment and horror as one of those covered wagons might have been a century and a half ago in Black Hawk's empire. But then Kish recognized the driver of the approaching car as Jim Taylor, the reporter for the Maryville newspaper, and waved him on. Now from way out in the corn came the sound of another siren—a Highway Patrol car was coming in on Road V.

While the attendants stood looking at the dead man and then looking away, Kish got on his police radio to relay the gory details to the sheriff's office in Maryville: *"It's McElroy all right—he's dead."* Taylor walked over to look at Ken Rex, then went over to talk to Kish. But there seemed to be nothing to say.

"It was pretty spooky," Taylor said later. "Nobody was around but the officers and the ambulance guys, but you got the feeling that people were watching from every window."

It stayed that way throughout the time the ambulance and patrol cars were there, while Kish began his preliminary investigation and Taylor began to put together his first story. Still the town was deserted.

By early afternoon many others would be there—the first fact finders and the morbidly curious. The shot-up truck remained on the street for a long time. Ken Rex's blood marked the killing ground. It had leaked out of the cab and down onto the pavement, making a stain about the size of a home plate. By next morning the stain would be gone—someone in Skidmore had come in the night and washed it away.

The ambulance brought the body back to St. Francis Hospital in Maryville, where what was left of Ken Rex was pronounced dead on arrival and carted over to the Price Funeral Home. Nodaway County Coroner Earl Siebert was out of town, so Buchanan County Medical Examiner Y. E. Silliman was called in to perform an autopsy.

The results of Silliman's examination weren't made public by Prosecutor Baird until late September, after the grand jury was dismissed, nearly three months after the murder. That autopsy revealed not only the massive rifle bullet wound to the back of Ken Rex's head, but also a small wound at the base of the neck on the right side, and two smaller wounds to the back of the neck that Silliman said could have been "consistent with gunshot wounds."

Silliman's statement about the two smaller wounds supported speculation that there might have been a second gunman—speculation that was further fueled by the report of ballistics experts who combed the scene in the first hours after the shooting. Their report said that in addition to the 8-millimeter Mauser rifle bullet casing found at the scene, several .22-caliber magnum hulls and one unspent .22-caliber magnum round were found.

There was really nothing to connect those .22-caliber leavings to the shooting of Ken Rex. There was no way to know how long they had been on the street before the investigation began—whether hours or days or months. There was no damage to the pickup that might have been caused by smaller-caliber bullets, and no .22 fragments were found either in the truck or in Ken Rex's body. Also, a magnum-force bullet has about twice the charge of a regular .22 bullet and probably would have caused more extensive damage than the small wounds that Silliman noted. Funeral home sources surmised that the neck wounds most likely were caused by flying glass.

In any case, the second-gunman question is incidental. It changes none of the main issues and even distracts from them. It was a marksman with a high-powered rifle who killed Ken Rex. Even that gunman's identity has little bearing on the meaning of the legend and legacy that still haunts Skidmore, still haunts us all.

Mabel Lister McElroy was a patient at St. Francis Hospital in Maryville when the ambulance arrived there with the bloody mess that had been the twelfth of her thirteen children. She had had a heart attack just a few days before and wasn't doing well. The last few years hadn't been kind to Mother Mabel; she was a widow (Tony McElroy had died five years ago) and in poor health, and her son's notoriety hadn't done much for her well-being. One of her other sons was with her in the hospital room, and so was Rev. Mike Smith.

Mike had just that week gotten his first pastoral assignment. He had moved to Maitland, six miles south of Skidmore, on Wednesday, and would fill the pulpit in Maitland and also conduct Sunday services at the Methodist church in Skidmore. Mike was making his first round of hospital visits and was there when a hospital attendant brought the news of the shooting.

160

AFTERMATH

"Ken Rex's been shot," the attendant burst in and said.

"What?" his brother asked. "Is he hurt bad?"

"He's dead."

The news and the sudden grief it caused almost killed Ken Rex's aged mother. Ken Rex had always been something of a pet child to her—"her cub," as a family friend described it. It was a relationship one often sees between a mother and a "problem child" who can't get along with his father. Mrs. McElroy had to be sedated on this day, but she was a Lister and a McElroy, of strong stock, and she would not only survive this shock but would get up out of her sickbed to be at Ken Rex's funeral, which Mike Smith would conduct.

The state of Missouri has a peculiar procedure for investigating major crimes involving special circumstances. It assembles what is called a Major Investigation Squad, made up of lawmen from the quadrant of the state in which the crime occurred, and these sheriffs, chiefs of police, and other law enforcement officials concentrate a lot of manpower on the scene quickly. The Northwest Missouri Investigation Squad (NOMIS), consisting of twenty-three officers and headed by Cameron Police Chief Hal Riddle, converged on Nodaway County during the evening of the same day that Ken Rex was shot. It set up headquarters in Maryville and took full control of the case, having been granted the authority to do so by the Nodaway County sheriff's office and the prosecuting attorney.

Among the first people the NOMIS investigators questioned at length was Sheriff Estes. They had some hard questions for the young lawman because he had attended

161

that big Legion Hall meeting in Skidmore, had heard the volatile talk there, had left town at a critical time, and hadn't arrived back at his office in the Maryville courthouse, thirteen miles away, until the noon-hour call was coming in that there had been a shooting in Skidmore at eleven o'clock.

They questioned Estes long into the night, and it isn't known what they learned from him because their subsequent report was never made public by Prosecutor Baird (the report was sealed by court order after the grand jury concluded its investigation). One thing they certainly learned, though, was that the case wasn't as simple as they might have supposed at first—it wasn't merely a matter of a shooting in broad daylight, with a whole town as eyewitness and no one talking.

Most of the NOMIS investigators hadn't planned to stay in Nodaway County beyond the weekend, but by Monday morning they had interviewed thirty-five Skidmore witnesses and had come up with nothing.

Hal Riddle had also found it necessary to assign one of his team to serve as a press information officer to handle the deluge of inquiries that poured in from newspapers, wire services, and television and radio stations and networks. The first news stories made national headlines because of the strong implication that a modern-day lynching had occurred in the classic frontier-justice style. As the Columbia (Mo.) *Daily Tribune* put it: "The vigilante killing in the frontier town has attracted the national news media."

Nodaway County was getting its first taste of American pack journalism, which works in much the same way as the locust and blackbird swarms that sometimes descend on small places in middle America. Newspaper reporters from St. Joseph, Kansas City, St. Louis, Des Moines, Chicago, and New York moved in almost as quickly as the NOMIS squad, as did the television crews from the national networks a few days later. Soon to follow was a greater wave of reporters for newspapers from Washington to Los Angeles; for magazines that ran the gamut from *Newsweek* and *People* to *Playboy* and *Rolling Stone;* for ABC and CBS and NBC. Dan Rather breezed in from New York to interview the widow, Trena, and Morley Safer came along a few weeks later with his *60 Minutes* entourage. Rather would devote whole segments of the evening news to the Skidmore incident, practically assuming that a modern-day lynching had occurred and calling for tough justice in the affair.

The crush of the media became so great that finally the editor of the Maryville *Daily Forum*, Tom Throne, would charge a consultation fee for interviews with Jim Taylor, the young reporter who was first on the scene. A lot of the bigwig journalists paid the fee.

Meanwhile Skidmore was mostly keeping its mouth shut and the NOMIS team was drawing a blank. So the bulk of the information in those early stories came from Trena and from McFadin in Kansas City. In an ironic statement that Skidmore relishes to this day, McFadin said the killing of Ken Rex represented "a complete breakdown of law and order."

Facts were hard to come by, and the vigilante motif, with nothing to dispute it, flourished in all the subsequent newspaper and magazine stories. Judgment Day at Skidmore became a distillation and amalgam of *High Noon*, *Death Wish*, and *Bad Day at Black Rock*, plus a dozen other famous showdowns and shoot-'em-ups. It could be made to fit them all.

Skidmore was astounded by all the attention and generally chagrined, although a few people, like Red Smith, the bartender at D&G's, seemed to enjoy it enormously. Skidmore was particularly incensed by a TV network report which used an artist's drawings showing a provincial mob completely surrounding the pickup and glowering murderously through its windows at a terrified Ken Rex. Ken Rex would have been as offended by those drawings as Skidmore was.

The first NOMIS press release, issued on Monday, July 13, 1981, three days after the killing, complained that the investigation which had begun with such confidence had "hit a dead end." An apt pun. All the promising early leads had evaporated. However many witnesses there had been at the scene, somehow none of them saw, heard, or remembered anything that was of any value at all.

The press release was significant because NOMIS had by this time interviewed Trena McElroy. And presumably she had told the investigators what she was telling reporters—that in those last panicky seconds before the shooting, she had seen a man standing behind the McElroy pickup with a gun. She said he was directly across the street from the tavern, no more than fifty feet from the pickup.

The investigators had also already interviewed this man, who soon thereafter went to another state and refused to comment publicly on the matter. NOMIS obviously chose to discount Trena's attempt to implicate him. That might have been because it had reconstructed the scene of the slaying and had concluded that the fatal shots came not from the spot where Trena said the man was standing, but from a different distance, a different location, and even a different angle. In her subsequent public statements about the shooting, Trena revealed a number of puzzling inconsistencies. She placed the crowd of watching men on one side of the truck, and then the other; she was confused about the number of gunshots; she spoke of the man as someone she "knew of but didn't know personally." All in all, the investigators eliminated him as a prime suspect.

With no prime suspect, the NOMIS team was stalemated and could only sit back and wait for some "concerned citizen" to come forward. By the end of their first week, the investigators were convinced that no such citizen would be coming.

*

Ken Rex's funeral, held at the Price Funeral Home chapel in Maryville on Tuesday, four days after the shooting, was a private service attended only by the family and close friends, though some reporters and photographers found their way into the chapel lobby.

Trena had come into Maryville that weekend to make the funeral arrangements. She wanted, among other things, an open casket during the service.

"We couldn't do that," the funeral director told her. "His head was just too badly torn up."

But Trena insisted, and the funeral director didn't know what else to do but call the minister who was to officiate at the service and ask him to speak to Trena.

"We need to convince her that it would be best to keep the casket closed, for the sake of the children if nothing else," the director told Rev. Mike Smith.

So Mike went out to the McElroy place, driving up to the house soon after dusk. When he got out of the car, he noticed the sign in the yard, GUARD DOGS ON DUTY. He heard some growls and snarls in the darkness and hesitated to approach the house.

Suddenly the front door banged open and three men rushed out onto the porch. One had a shotgun and he aimed it just over Mike's head and fired. Mike sprawled on the ground and began to yelp piteously:

"Don't shoot me! Don't shoot me! I'm the preacher!"

The men came down from the porch and surrounded him. The one with the gun aimed it at his head and said, "You don't look like no preacher to me."

In his casual dress, the young man really didn't look much like a preacher, and his life flashed before his eyes before Trena stepped out on the front porch and approved the visitor.

"That's the preacher," she said. "He's all right. I'm expecting him."

Mike was able to persuade Trena to keep the casket closed, and the funeral took place on Tuesday without incident. The pallbearers were some of Ken Rex's drinking buddies and fellow coon-dog fanciers. Both Trena and Alice Woods were there with their children and some of Ken Rex's other offspring. Mabel Lister McElroy was there with her youngest son, Tim. In all, fewer than thirty people attended the service.

Some of the men appeared to be carrying weapons under their jackets, the result of another ironic twist to this story. The McElroys and their friends were now reporting that they were receiving anonymous threats. One of these friends had found an unsigned note in his mailbox: "Our bellies are full of your kind. Ken did not pay attention to leave the country when told to. Get out of this territory while you can. You have been warned. We don't want any thieves or rustlers or troublemakers."

AFTERMATH

The service lasted only about fifteen minutes. Mike Smith read the appropriate dust-to-dust Scriptures and spoke a few words of consolation to the family. He didn't mention the dead man's name.

Shortly thereafter, a cortege left the funeral home for the forty-five-minute midafternoon drive down to St. Joseph, where Trena had arranged for a burial site in Memorial Park Cemetery.

At the cemetery, the preacher read a few more verses of Scripture and then the casket was lowered into the earth. The funeral director said the whole family seemed genuinely bereaved. Both widows wept. So did the children and Mother Mabel.

A dozen daisies flanked the metal marker, which bore the simplest and most enigmatic of inscriptions:

KEN REX MCELROY
1934   1981

What did these grieving people think of Ken Rex's life and his death as the casket dropped him into the ground?

"A farm owner," his obituary had called him. He had been a farmer in a way. He had planted and harvested more hate than any other man in the Nodaway Empire. He had sown the wind and reaped the whirlwind. It was hate that killed him, but it was love expressed in grief that now committed him to the earth.

Maybe the benedictory Scripture that Mike Smith read should have been the seventh verse of the thirteenth chapter of First Corinthians, which characterizes love as that which "beareth all things, believeth all things, hopeth all things, and endureth all things."

His mother knew what Ken Rex was and probably she alone among these mourners endured the sure, sad knowledge of how he came to be the way he was. Her love for him was the enduring kind, in spite of and because of everything.

Trena's love affair with Ken Rex was born in violence, persisted in the shadow of violence, and died in violence. She endured a lot to love him, but her love in the end was the believing kind. She believed in him as he could never believe in himself. To himself, to others, Ken Rex had to prove himself over and over, relentlessly, even fatally, but not to Trena. She believed that the Ken Rex that he always wanted to be actually was. Maybe that's why they were always so close.

The other wife, Alice, stayed with him until the end, too, having dutifully moved over into that strange, reviled, auxiliary role that must have been an eternal heartbreak to her, for she had to watch as he bestowed whatever sparse, rough romance he had in him on Trena. Alice's love was the bearing kind.

And the love of the children was the hoping kind—the trusting kind, really. They trusted as only children can that the father they knew was the man familiar to them, and not the ogre that others spoke of.

The McElroy children were said to have been greatly disturbed by the murder of their father. The house wailed during the small hours from their nightmares. Ken Rex's son Juarez, who was thirteen, went so far as to tattoo with a needle the word "Dad" on his right arm. It was no superficial tattoo either, and to underscore it all he added the tattoo of a dagger just below his needlework. Juarez's gesture was a laborious and painful tribute that he will wear conspicuously the rest of his life.

One wonders about a youngster like that. Will he get the schooling and breaks needed to become the somebody his father and his father's father tried so desperately to be through brutishness and braggadocio? At his age, Juarez's father had already quit school, had already had his first brushes with the law, and was already well on his way to becoming the Ken Rex who would not be able to live as anything else. This child has inherited a legend, but it isn't the same legend—not exactly—that haunts the main street of Skidmore. He loved his Dad. Will he, out of a sense of obligation, let that love make the circle back to hate—so that once again something will be in the Nodaway air, something ominous and troubling, building, until the curse touches down again? Will he create his own Skidmore?

Trena and Alice picked up and moved the day after the funeral. They eventually wound up in a small town near St. Joe, where they faced the great task of keeping their improbable family together. Trena's grief soon took a practical turn. She put an advertisement in the Maryville newspaper offering a five-thousand-dollar reward for information leading to the conviction of Ken Rex's killer. The reward money would come from the bonanza she expected to receive from the sale of the movie rights to "her story."

It's interesting to imagine what such a movie, filmed from her point of view, might be like. Doubtless it would reflect Ken Rex's view, only without that crucial, fate-haunted intuition that made him such a formidable, frightening, and, finally, tragic villain. Would he even be an outlaw in this movie—or would he be portrayed as a much maligned, misunderstood farmer, antiques dealer, and devoted family man? Would houses burst into flame to his amazement and other farmers' cattle and pigs tear down gates and fences in order to climb into his stock trailer at two o'clock in the morning? Would Skidmore's womenfolk be panting with sexual fantasies about him while their vigilante menfolk glared into that pickup in just the way depicted in the TV artist's rendering?

Well, Hollywood can do wonders with a legend.

*

The NOMIS squad, meantime, kept trying. A week after the killing it suddenly announced that it was making good progress. Something had broken at Skidmore, and it was getting cooperation and some promising new leads.

The national reporters on the scene were also now finding more people in Skidmore who were willing to talk. What was going on?

Shrewd little Skidmore had realized that its silence had become counter-productive. The headlines (for example, THE MAN THEY HATED TO DEATH) were making the town look bad. Trena was getting big press, complaining that nothing was being done in the case, berating the NOMIS investigators for ignoring her testimony, and recounting the ordeal she had undergone on the day of the murder.

And the professional deplorers and expressers of shock were getting in some good licks. John Ashcroft, the state attorney general, issued a statement to the press in which he compared the shooting to a lynching and furthermore declared that "vigilantism has to be stopped at all costs." McFadin, threatening legal action, said he was considering a wrongful-death suit against Del Clement and added that he might even charge the "whole town" of Skidmore with complicity.

The nature of Skidmore's long struggle with Ken Rex

had changed again. It was now a struggle for public opinion, and Skidmore was getting the worse of it. Even dead, Ken Rex was giving Skidmore the dickens.

So Skidmore got its story together during that week of silence, and now it began to talk. It resurrected for reporters the Ken Rex horror stories of old and no doubt embellished them considerably. It even invented some new ones, some of which have since worked their way into the legend: how Ken Rex had gotten seventeen different girls pregnant in one year, had killed a dozen men around the territory, and was smuggling dope for the mob and using the livestock he stole merely as a cover. Skidmore was obviously scattering false scents to occupy and entertain the investigators.

There probably wasn't any conscious community collusion involved in this "betterment" project, although it later became known the townspeople had decided that, in the event NOMIS charged one of them in the killing, dozens of other Skidmore men would surrender to the authorities and confess to having pulled the trigger. They would all come forward:

"I did it, I shot Ken Rex."
"No, he didn't do it, I did!"
"You're crazy as hell. I'm the one who did it."
"You're all crazy! I'm the one who pulled the trigger."

Skidmore's new tactics began to have some effect. The headlines began to tilt ever so slightly in Skidmore's favor (TO THE KILLER OF HER LEAST FAVORITE SON, SKIDMORE SAYS A LONG SILENT THANK-YOU). News stories now were focusing on the discrepancies in Trena's accounts and on the little town's long years of suffering under the "bully's" oppression.

So the deplorers had to start sharing the limelight with

171

the anti-deplorers, as when Kenneth Rothman, the Missouri lieutenant governor, told reporters: "It was unfortunate that a crime was committed. On the other hand, you can't allow a community to be terrorized. It must have been a desperate situation." Even the Maryville *Daily Forum* editorialized that "the residents of Skidmore were genuinely afraid of McElroy" and went on to say sympathetically that Skidmore felt "law enforcement officials were not doing anything to help their situation." And when the NOMIS team ended its investigation a few days later, it did so with no criticism of Skidmore.

Skidmore's efforts to justify itself ultimately served only to magnify the legend of Ken Rex. If the widows had portrayed Ken Rex as a martyred hero, a corn country version of Big Bad John, then Skidmore had made him into a monster. In either rendering, he was larger than life, so covered with lore that it became impossible and even pointless to assess the numerous tales about his exploits and offenses. The courthouse sheltered the few unrevealing records of his life and death, but most of the drama of his life and death had been played out in people's minds. Those keepers of his memory all had their motives, so the fact finders, official and unofficial, were at a loss.

Ten days after the killing—on the day when Ken Rex would have had his bond-revocation hearing and probably would have gone to jail—the NOMIS team officially gave up its investigation. It declared the work a success, and its twenty-three officers closed their notebooks and pocketed their pens and went home. They had made no arrests, were not even close to any, and had no likely suspects. They made a report to the Missouri Highway Patrol and handed the case back to the Nodaway County authorities—to Sheriff Estes and Prosecutor Baird, who surely didn't want it.

The great struggle that had taken place in Skidmore had whispered one word every time it brushed up against the courthouse in Maryville. That word was "failure." The courthouse and the system of justice it represented had failed to protect Skidmore from Ken Rex, and it had failed to protect Ken Rex from Skidmore. Ken Rex, in his heyday, had known that the courthouse was nothing to worry about, and Skidmore finally learned that lesson from him.

Skidmore was not worried now, not in the least. For years the courthouse had tried to pretend that the struggle in Skidmore didn't exist. Its officer was nowhere to be seen as the struggle reached its crisis. And the courthouse had washed its hands of the whole messy affair by turning the murder investigation over to a team of outsiders.

But now, ten days after the killing, it had the case back. With the world looking on, it had no idea what to do with it. Ken Rex draped that courthouse as he had draped that steering wheel—like an albatross. A politician, finding himself so burdened, is likely to share the burden as extensively as possible. So Sheriff Estes called a coroner's jury and Prosecutor Baird prepared to call a grand jury.

The coroner's jury, composed of six men from different communities in the county, met for two days, weighed the old evidence, and called some of the same witnesses. This time Nodaway's coroner, Earl Siebert, was in town and he presided over the inquest. Appearing before the jury first was Jim Kish of the sheriff's department. Kish told the jury what he had discovered when he went out to Skidmore that July morning—a deserted town and a man dead in a pickup truck. Others testifying before the jury were

173

JUDGMENT DAY

Steve Peter, Jim Hartman, Howard Kenny, and Red Smith, all of Skidmore and all on the scene at the time of the shooting. All said they had seen nothing.

The coroner's jury issued a brief statement saying there was "almost" enough evidence for a warrant but not enough for an arrest. That was presumably intended to convey the impression that the courthouse authorities weren't just thrashing around in the dark.

Which of course they were.

The FBI out of Kansas City, which had quietly launched its own investigation and was nosing around for evidence of a conspiracy, added to the tremendous pressure that the courthouse felt from the intense media scrutiny. The pressure eased a bit when the grand jury—the first in Nodaway County in thirteen years—went into session on August 10, exactly a month after Judgment Day. Since the grand jury's deliberations are kept secret, no one could say that the authorities of Nodaway County weren't making a vigorous effort to break the McElroy case.

Smiling inscrutably at reporters and expressing optimism that the jury would endorse a bill of indictment, Prosecutor Baird made headlines each time he went in and out of the jury's chambers. His wonderful outward glow spoke for the good old system of justice that was presumably working ever so smoothly.

And the sheriff's office turned into such a model of business and serious demeanor that it might have been an elaborate life-sized model of a Swiss clock. The Corps of Engineers couldn't have done it better.

Skidmore, meanwhile, celebrated its Punkin Festival in late August, and according to all reports, it was a huge success. The Maryville *Daily Forum* carried a front-page feature on the event, accompanied by a picture of the cute little Punkin Queen, Kelli Strauch.

The theme of the festival was "Movin' with America." Skidmore postmaster Jim Hartman said that a large crowd turned out in spite of the rain. Activities for the four-day festival included a variety show, square dancing, a rock concert, horseshoe pitching, a meat auction, a flea market, fireworks display, and a baby show. A big parade went through downtown Skidmore on Saturday afternoon, with a special appearance by Smokey the Bear. On Sunday morning, Reverend Tim Warren and Reverend Mike Smith conducted a community worship service on the school grounds. The festival concluded Sunday afternoon with boat races down the Nodaway River. Proceeds from the show went to the Skidmore Betterment Club and the fire department.

Just about everybody in Skidmore agreed that it was the best Punkin Festival ever. And if anyone there had expressed undue concern about the foofaraw over at Maryville's courthouse, he would have been laughed halfway over to Tarkio.

The grand jury kept at it, plowing the same sterile ground that the professionals had already exhausted. A clerk in the courthouse summed up the prevailing view when she told a reporter: "Oh, the grand jury's not meeting again today—for lack of interest."

*

Fall came.

And as always, its coming was a thing of grandeur in the Nodaway Empire.

The sticky heat gave way to the cool air drifting down

over the Black Hills from Canada. The weather was mostly dry and good for haying and harvesting. The corn was in, and the fields, lapping up over the rims of those immense saucers, began to fade slowly from deep green to brilliant amber. Squat pumpkins oranged up in the gardens and hogs gobbed up for the impending slaughterhouse weigh-ins. The leaves on the big shade trees along Skidmore's main street started turning red and gold. A formation of high-flying wild geese suggested another source for the curt name of incoming County Road V.

The Skidmore nights, untroubled now, were bright with stars that city dwellers seldom get to see. Only the skull of the harvest moon asked questions.

Then, on the verge of October, the grand jury gave it up too. It appeared to simply get tired of meeting for the sake of having meetings. Up to the last minute the prosecutor had seemed very confident that the jury would hand down a true bill. But all they handed down were their jurors' lapel pins.

On that same day the prosecutor told a battery of reporters that he wouldn't push for further action in the case because there was obviously no evidence against anyone "beyond a reasonable doubt." He suggested that the news media had blown the case all out of proportion, and he discounted the Ken Rex legend as "a fabrication of the national press."

He was whistling an old tune, one that Skidmore had come to know well enough to rely on and that should provide more theme music to this story without an end.

The last note to this particular verse was sounded by an editorial in the Maryville *Daily Forum:*

"Those who believe the Grand Jury has failed apparently do not understand the difference between failure and success of our legal system. The fact is that the grand jury was immensely successful in sifting through hearsay and gossip to arrive at a conclusion . . ."

What a remarkable statement that is!

Just as the NOMIS team had declared its investigation a success, so now the fiduciary voice of the Nodaway Empire declared the grand jury's investigation a success. And not just an ordinary success but an *immense* success—a success of such magnitude as to exculpate the entire legal system. The jury's deliberations were secret, but obviously "hearsay and gossip" had been "sifted." A "conclusion" had been arrived at. The message was that anybody who didn't think that represented an immense success, "just didn't understand."

Skidmore understood, all right, having learned the hard way from old master Ken Rex what all the self-serving mumbo jumbo and legalistic rigmarole would amount to. Skidmore had draped the carcass of Ken Rex over the courthouse dome—had hung it around the neck of the legal system that courthouse represented—and like Ken Rex in his heyday, listening with amusement to the police scanner in his Chevy pickup, Skidmore sat back now and enjoyed the show.

The editorial ended by expressing the hope that "the case will be vigorously pursued." It didn't suggest how or by whom. The prosecuting attorney had already announced that he wasn't going to pursue it through any further legal channels, and it wasn't very likely that the sheriff's department would take any other action short of declining to appear before any more "concerned citizens' " forums or town meetings.

The FBI continued to poke around, sealing up records

and giving folks reason to wonder if the next step might not be the impaneling of a federal grand jury. But everybody knew the FBI didn't have its heart in this one. McFadin, who never got around to filing that wrongful-death lawsuit, talked about other actions he might take, but these days he was an awfully busy man and stayed in his big-city province, taking care of business.

Reporters came back from time to time to write follow-up stories and summaries. Skidmore received congratulatory letters from all over the country, addressed in most cases "To Whom It May Concern." No one was lured by Trena's IOU reward offer.

Later in the fall, the McElroy murder case, for all practical purposes, was closed. A federal grand jury was, indeed, convened in Kansas City. Though its findings would be the same as other investigative bodies', its verdict wouldn't be handed down until spring. The FBI announced, too, that it was "calling off the dogs."

The Nodaway Empire braced itself for another raw winter; it began to yawn and nod away.

The Road Back

"There's no question of heroism in all
this. It's a matter of common decency."
　　—from *The Plague* by Albert Camus

As winter moved in from the Great Plains, the factfinders
slowly vanished from the scene, and the unfinished struggle between Ken Rex and Skidmore returned to that dark
place that exists timelessly in the mind. That's where it
belonged—not in the courthouse or out on the street or
in the newspapers. Not out there in the light where the
mysteries of life are poked and probed and scrutinized
and diagnosed so they can be explained, adjudged, and
disposed of. In that dark place, the strugglers were
legends now—not only Ken Rex but Skidmore too, Skidmore in the form into which it had coalesced and mani-
fested itself for just a few hours on the morning of July 10,
1981—and their struggle was a myth in the making.

179

It still is.

So if the factfinders have vanished, then one must also take the road back. But there is still something in the air that makes one stay—a desire to find one last *fact* for one-self, at least one clue to the unanswered question. Maybe that clue is conveyed in the sound of the wind over the eaves of the little town, like the muted cry of a siren pulling one back to a hot July day.

Then everything goes grainy again, with the silence of the town too pithy, the street too crusty, and things in general lulling one back into the old comforting detachment. The answer is here—it can be felt—but the clue lies elsewhere. Because this town, where recently a mind-less pageant took place and the old curse touched down for a moment—is as impervious as the old hawk that wings over its heartland.

And so the search must be carried elsewhere. One must draw back from this perspective and instead view the well-made, purely sculptured landscape through the eyes of that vagabond hawk.

The native place has the look of everything midwest-ern—it is neat, unpretentious, comfortable. The house sits atop one of those rolls and looks down across the fair-est view in the Nodaway Empire. It is just a few miles southeast of Maryville, across maybe half a score of those glacial rolls from Skidmore, but as far away too as the buf-falo. Hardly any of the factfinders ventured out this way—it was too far off Ken Rex's beaten path.

John Middleton, longtime sheriff of Nodaway County, lives here with his wife, Helen, in simple retirement. John is a short, heavyset bull of a man who gives the impression he's not afraid of any man and doesn't give a tinker's damn what he says even in polite company. He's a talker and it's too bad the factfinders didn't seek him out. He could have put some light on the subject they were researching.

The more you're with John, the more you wonder if he doesn't hold the key to the mystery that was Ken Rex. John had known Ken Rex well, maybe better than any other man in the territory. Tony and Mabel McElroy had counted John Middleton as their friend, and he had watched all their children grow up. He had especially kept his eye on the troubled boy, Kenny.

So every conversation with John Middleton eventually comes down to the question: *Who was Ken Rex?* He supplies no direct answers, and maybe that's because there was some sort of unspoken agreement between the two men, or at least an understanding of the sort that sometimes exists between outlaw and lawman.

Listening to John talk about those distressing early years and the growing legend of Ken Rex, one begins to grasp a little of the meaning behind the enigma. John has more stories to contribute to the legend, but one feels one can trust them. They are stories about Ken Rex's brutishness and show the way he taunted and bullied men and brutalized women. But there are other stories, too, which reveal a different, almost childlike quality in the man. Over the years John had had many run-ins with Ken Rex; he had had to arrest him several times. And he rarely had trouble with the man so many other lawmen feared to go near: "If I wanted to arrest him or talk to him, I'd just call him up and say, 'Ken, get your ass in here to my office.' And he'd come on in. You had to stand up to him for him to respect you."

One time, John was on his way to one of Ken Rex's trials

when he saw Ken Rex and his lawyer sitting on the top steps of the courthouse. John walked by, spoke, and when they didn't respond, he circled back around them and pointed his finger and said, "By God, I spoke to you! When I speak to somebody, I expect him to answer me back." Ken Rex looked up then, as though just noticing the sheriff, and replied softly, "Oh, hi, John."

Other stories too show a softer side to the man. Ken Rex once gave a car to an old man who was so poor he had to walk everywhere he went. And once at a sale-barn auction Ken Rex gave an expensive watch to a man who had simply asked him the time. There was a purpose to Ken Rex's generosity, John Middleton says. "He liked to be the big man. He *had* to be the big man. He always showed off, especially in front of kids. He'd tease them and buy them some pop and give them money. He'd tell them what a big man he was. He always carried a gun, and he'd show it off in front of the kids. That's what Ken Rex wanted to be, the top gun."

After hours of talk about Ken Rex and the law and the little town of Skidmore, one can't help making some sort of a comparison: Both John Middleton and Ken Rex McElroy were outwardly strong, with the tough physical presence of bullies. Both commanded respect, but one did it by being admired and the other by being feared and loathed. Both were poorly educated, but possessed high levels of native intelligence and uncanny intuition. But John had no inner turmoil, no killing self-doubts; he used his native gift to assist people in a positive way, whereas Ken Rex applied his toward bending and training dogs and people to his will. It is no coincidence, one feels, that as long as John was in office, the "problem" of Ken Rex was somewhat under control. In a way, the old sheriff functioned as Ken Rex's limiter and locus-of-control. It may be more than an assumption to say that the greatest psychological event of Ken Rex's life was John Middleton's retirement—for it was only after then that Ken Rex embarked upon his notorious and self-destructive crusade.

At the end of a visit with John Middleton out on his hillside, the talk comes back once more to the bad thing that happened over in Skidmore. You've been wanting to ask something for a long time, something for your benefit instead of his, but maybe for the benefit of everybody who still searches for the answer to the question. After the question has been put, there's a pause, as if he's reading your thoughts, and the words go unsaid.

But this much is plain: This tough old bird of a lawman would have caught the scent of whatever was in the air on that day in July 1981. Had he been there as sheriff that day, you think to yourself . . . and then you let that idea go too, for it's pointless now.

John Middleton merely grins, as if brushing the unspoken thought aside. He leans forward, his eyes bright with that keen native sense of his, and says almost in a whisper:

"If you ask me, the way they did it, the whole business, was done with a lot of bad taste."

The hoary-headed old hawk rises from his solemn perch in a bare sycamore tree, beats his way upward until he is gliding strongly with the upper air currents, and begins to survey his domain. He knows it is his territory, for he's a sovereign, too, like that obstinate old monarch who once ruled here, that last emperor who was called by the same name.

JUDGMENT DAY

A few miles east of John Middleton's place, the country-side grows even neater and cleaner. The little towns are immaculate, with their combed, clipped, and manicured fields and yards.

In these parts one comes upon a community that looks as out of place as Macbeth's castle would. It is the Catholic abbey, with its cathedral, pretty grounds, and cupular groves. Down a hillside lies a printery that does a booming business in greeting cards.

Father Alphonse has charge of the printery. He's a rotund, pleasant man of about forty-five, with a ready smile for all those who come his way. None of the factfinders came his way, though he is probably the nearest thing to an intellectual that the Nodaway Empire has to offer.

Alphonse is also a zestful man. When you meet him, he will likely be eating a cookie and telling a joke. He'll lead a visitor through the printshop and into his office, which is tastefully elegant, with its walnut desk and hundreds of books lining the walls. He'll probably want to talk books—both best sellers and the classics—while the visitor sips some of the abbey's fine wine.

"Most people believe the killing was justified," he has said. "And you know why? They probably had never seen this man McElroy in their lives, but they want to believe such a story. There is no way you can justify the taking of a life, but people want to believe there is some hope against beasts . . ."

*

All winter a white stillness deepens and holds the land. Skidmore rests on its hill, waiting for sun and green. Soon the Nodaway River will be melting apace. The thaw-crack

184

of spring can already almost be heard coming across those glazed glacial rolls.

Nothing much happens in the bleak months. This year people count that a blessing. Now and then farmers take winter stock to market. The basketball team of the nearby Nodaway consolidated high school has its ups and downs. Highline wires freeze up and knock out power for half a day. And Skidmore occupies itself by worrying about its kids, wondering if they're drinking or trying out drugs. A commune of young people living a couple miles out of town in trailers forms a band; they play mostly soft music and are well received in the area—they even get invited to play a lounge gig in Vegas.

All along the main street the maples and nut trees shiver and swell and want badly to start budding. Through the winter months the street stays mostly deserted, but now and then a pickup cruises into town and guys get out and go into D&G's to drink beer—the coldest beer in the world and still only sixty cents on tap. The tavern is under new management now and has been upgraded somewhat, even to offering fresh shrimp. The jukebox stands silent against the far wall, close to the place where Ken Rex used to station himself. But now the guys talk sports instead of guns and threats. A Ping-Pong and pool tournament will highlight the bleak days, for the challenge has gone out to Maitland, six miles down the road. This time the women have been invited to take part.

Yet the struggle continues and the question persists. What did it mean, this growing myth of a midsummer mid-America showdown between a man now moldering in his grave and a little town now going about its uneventful business as the snow flies?

JUDGMENT DAY

Like all great myths, this one is a web of tragic misunderstanding.

Skidmore thought it was struggling against Ken Rex, a brute and a thug, but it was really struggling to reclaim its own heart, which is the heart not just of a town but of a country and a culture and an epoch. There was lethargy in that heart where vitality should have been. There was a flabby will that had come to accept the unacceptable and tolerate the intolerable. There was a failure of commitment that had been responsible for letting Ken Rex become what he had become. There was a lost quality, a sense of drift . . .

But when Skidmore sucked in its gut and walked into that tavern and looked an old terror in the eye, it reclaimed its heart, and the victory was a great one, not just for an out-of-the-way hamlet, but for civilized behavior and human decency. Skidmore looked a legend in the eye, and the Lord of the Night turned out to be only a bloated loser, just as the Lord of the Flies turned out to be nothing more than a pig's head on the end of a stick.

But the gods are jealous of human triumphs, and they exact a heavy price for them. They let Skidmore have this triumph for only as long as it took a gunman to squeeze off two rounds. Then they transformed it into tragedy, stained it with blood, mocked it with gore, and shamed it in the eyes of the law and of civilization.

They saw to it that Ken Rex remained out there on the street—amid the shattered glass and bloody gore under the noonday sun—not for just an hour, but for good. They left him out there as a way of saying, "Here's what comes of your pride, your self-righteousness, your perversion of the Christianity you avow. Here's your trophy. Live with it now."

THE ROAD BACK

Ken Rex, too, thought his struggle was against other people when it was against himself. His opponent was the puffy, ailing, aging, no-longer-intimidating fat man, doomed to end up in prison or else to mend his wild and wicked ways, a man who would never be able to resolve the conflict that raged inside him and never be able to prove to himself whatever impossible thing he had devoted his life to proving. He knew what was in the air on that final morning. It was Death calling him out. And when he walked out of the tavern, he wasn't walking away from a confrontation with Skidmore. He was walking toward the showdown of his life. Death made him wait, teasing him, tormenting him in his own terrifying style, as he sat with his thumb and forefinger on that ignition key. But he, too, won his victory. He gained apotheosis even though the deed was done in bad taste and out of desperation in a hopeless struggle against beasts. His was no less a victory than Skidmore's, and it lasted just about as long and cost him his life.

The struggle goes on, and we're all in the thick of it, struggling blindly.

The myth accompanies a visitor as he leaves Skidmore, going back along the road by which he came.

He follows the roll and swale of County Road V, noting the way the encircling landscape has gone gray and umber now in the grip of winter, and then somewhere out near White Cloud Creek he glances back toward the little town that perches on the track of a glacier.

What he sees is so arresting that he will bring it back with him. It's a view of the sky over Skidmore, with a decrepit windmill nearby, its broken blades clacking mournfully in the cold wind.

JUDGMENT DAY

The sky is indigo and the first stars are out. The sun has set, but its last rays linger on the underbelly of a cloud bank towering over Skidmore, turning it as scarlet as sin itself.

And from the east, bisecting the sky and following the arc of its dome, the vapor trail of a westbound jetliner leads the eye to the gleaming mote that is the plane itself. Because of the curvature of the earth, the plane appears to be going down, not away. It appears to be plunging down into that scarlet cloud bank, down into the heart of Skidmore, Missouri, U.S.A.

Its silver plunge evokes the image of an Indian's arrow, or the dagger which Juarez McElroy tattooed on his forearm just below the needle track that spells out "Dad."